TEXAS WATER ATLAS

RIVER BOOKS

Sponsored by

 the River Systems Institute
at Texas State University

Andrew Sansom,

General Editor

TEXAS WATER ATLAS

LAWRENCE E. ESTAVILLE
AND **RICHARD A. EARL**

PREFACE BY ANDREW SANSOM

TEXAS A&M UNIVERSITY PRESS   College Station

This paper meets the requirements of
ANSI/NISO Z39.48-1992 (Permanence of Paper).
Binding materials have been chosen for durability.
∞

Library of Congress Cataloging-in-Publication Data

Estaville, Lawrence E. (Lawrence Ernest)
    Texas water atlas / Lawrence E. Estaville and Richard A.
Earl ; preface by Andrew Sansom.
       p. cm. — (River books)
    Includes bibliographical references and index.
    ISBN-13: 978-1-60344-020-2 (cloth : alk. paper)
    ISBN-10: 1-60344-020-8 (cloth : alk. paper)
    1. Hydrology—Texas. 2. Hydrology—Texas—Maps.
3. Hydrology—Texas—Pictorial works. I. Earl, Richard A.
(Richard Allen) II. Title.
GB705.T4E88 2008
553.709764—dc22
                                                                  2007033914

To Sandra Estaville and Karen Earl

Contents

Preface

This book is the logical product of years of excellence in geography and water resource studies at Texas State University, and I am privileged to have been a small part of that evolution. When I began to think about leaving my job at Texas Parks and Wildlife during the first year of the new century, I really wasn't ready to retire and felt that an academic setting would provide me with a meaningful opportunity to share with young people what knowledge I might have accumulated and to continue working on natural resource issues and other challenges of interest to me. At that time, my colleague Gilbert Grosvenor, chairman of the National Geographic Society, told me the best geography department in the country was located thirty miles south of Austin on the campus of what was then Southwest Texas State University. Indeed, the undergraduate geography program at Texas State has grown to become the largest in America and the department now boasts two master's degrees and three Ph.D. degrees as well.

A good measure of this success is due to former geography department chairman Lawrence Estaville, coauthor of this first-ever *Texas Water Atlas*. Estaville and Richard Earl, a leading water expert from the geography faculty, have produced an essential reference for those who seek a deeper understanding of one of the most crucial issues of our time. In the pages of this volume of the River Books series—a collaborative enterprise of the River Systems Institute at Texas State University and the Texas A&M University Press—scholars, policymakers, water professionals, activists, and anyone interested in Texas' most critical natural resource will find an indispensable tool for understanding the circulatory system of the Lone Star State.

Understand it we must, for it is now clear that providing sufficient water for the health of our people, for continued economic growth, and for the environment will be the most daunting challenge we have faced in Texas in many years. We do not have a choice but to address these challenges, and doing so requires a broad perspective of water as an issue of climate, location, distribution, and consumption. Estaville and Earl here offer a geo-spatial context for our use which provides this perspective. Their work has been aided by another Texas supporter of geographers, Marilyn Oshman of Houston, and we are grateful for all that she does for us and for the natural resources of Texas.

In the years ahead, particularly given the changes which are taking place in our climate, the issue of our water supply will occupy an ever greater share of our time, energy, money, and imagination. Thankfully, there are scholars like Lawrence Estaville and Richard Earl who can provide us with pathways to understanding and solutions, and there are universities like Texas State that support such work as a core value. I feel privileged to be part of the team.

—Andrew Sansom

Acknowledgments

The Texas Atlas Project in the Department of Geography at Texas State University–San Marcos created the *Texas Water Atlas*. We thank Kristine Egan, atlas production manager, and the production staff composed of John McLaughlin, Rachel Benke, and Jeff Sun for their excellent work in gathering pertinent data and drafting the atlas maps. Kristine Egan also provided some of the photographs for the atlas.

We appreciate the Department of Geography and the River Systems Institute at Texas State University–San Marcos for funding components of the production of the *Texas Water Atlas*. We are grateful to Andrew Sansom, executive director of the River Systems Institute, and Angelika Wahl, office manager for the Texas State Geography Department, for their steadfast encouragement as we worked for many months to produce the atlas. We also thank James R. Kimmel, Texas State Geography Department and coauthor of *San Marcos: A River's Story;* Helen C. Besse, Capital Environmental Services; and A. Kim Ludeke, Texas Parks and Wildlife; as well as Shannon Davies at Texas A&M University Press and copyeditor Cynthia H. Lindlof for their insightful suggestions that strengthened our work.

Introduction

Water is essential for life. Abundant, reliable, and high-quality water resources are necessary for the health of humans and wildlife and for agricultural and economic development. Texans need to have critical information about and a fundamental understanding of their water resources if the state is to prosper. To help reach this essential goal, the *Texas Water Atlas* is a unique educational guide.

The *Texas Water Atlas* is organized into seven chapters that feature more than 150 color maps and graphics highlighting the state's climate, water resources and hazards, and projections for future water needs. The Texas Water Timeline traces water uses and hazards principally of European settlements through the state's current water challenges, and a glossary explains key terms and frequently used abbreviations for governmental agencies. Accompanying the *Texas Water Atlas* is a County Data Table that focuses on future water projections and pollution sources and can be freely downloaded from www.geo .txstate/texasatlasproject/texaswaterdata.

Chapter 1 of the *Texas Water Atlas* details the state's *climate*, which is so important to producing the water that fills Texas rivers and aquifers. Chapter 2 paints the patterns of *surface water and groundwater* resources that have been fought over for decades and for which different legal frameworks exist. *Water hazards*, as elucidated in chapter 3, seriously affect humans and ecosystems, as floods and droughts pummel Texas all too frequently. Chapter 4 illuminates how Texans have dealt with imperative *water quantity and quality issues*. Important Texas *water projects*, major sources of *water pollution* in the state, and the agencies that have responsibility to *protect* the precious water resources are the central themes of chapter 5. Chapter 6 celebrates *water recreation* and the fun times that Texans have in enjoying the state's large variety of water bodies. The state's *water prospects* are charted in chapter 7 through an array of water supply projections that incorporate the future demands of a rapidly growing population for Texas water.

TEXAS WATER ATLAS

1 Climate

AVAILABLE WATER SUPPLY IS DIRECTLY controlled by precipitation and temperature, two of the major factors that define climate. Usable water is what remains of precipitation after evaporation and use by vegetation through the process of transpiration. Because temperatures control the amounts of both evaporation and transpiration, seasonal variations of usable water may be considerable.

The large size and geographic location of Texas cause the state's climates to range from arid to humid in a west-to-east direction, and from cold-winter continental steppe in the north to subtropical in the south. El Paso in far West Texas has less than 10 inches mean annual precipitation. Precipitation increases in a west-to-east direction at approximately 1 inch for roughly every 15 miles so that mean annual precipitation at Port Arthur along the Louisiana border is greater than 55 inches (NOAA 2002; NCDC 2000). The major controls for this precipitation pattern are proximity to Gulf of Mexico moisture, mountain barriers in the west, the increasing blocking action of the subtropical high-pressure cell toward the west, and the march of winter frontal boundaries through the state. In other words, the climates of Texas are caused mainly by external factors rather than those within the state. To minimize the variations of data gathered at its weather stations, the U.S. National Weather Service divides Texas into ten climatic divisions (NWS 1959).

Determining the amount of available water at a particular location is complicated by difficulties in measuring evaporation and transpiration. Collectively, evaporation and transpiration are termed "evapotranspiration." Actual evapotranspiration (AE) means exactly that—the actual amount of water that is evapotranspired from a site. Potential evapotranspiration (PET) is the amount of water that could be evapotranspired if it were available. Potential evapotranspiration is important because it is the amount of water required for optimal plant growth, a fundamental concept in irrigation. Too little water and plant growth is inhibited. Too much water leads to expensive water being wasted and agricultural chemicals unnecessarily washed away. Significantly influencing the process of evapotranspiration are air temperature, surface temperature, atmospheric humidity, wind, and sunshine. Of these controls, only temperature data are available for most weather stations. The lack of data for the other influencing factors poses major problems for developing methods of calculating potential evapotranspiration.

C. W. Thornthwaite (1948) developed early methods for calculating PET that were later updated by other climate researchers, most notably by the Priestly Taylor Method. The Thornthwaite model calculated PET as a function of air temperature, date in the year, and latitude. Because the model does not incorporate data for the amount of sunshine, wind, and low humidity, it substantially underestimates PET in dry, windy, sunny locations such as West Texas (Dunne and Leopold 1978). Later methods more accurately measure PET. H. L. Penman developed one of the most commonly used methods that incorporates a "crop factor" coefficient to accommodate the distinct water needs of different types of plants (Dingman 2002; Jenson, Burman, and Allen 1992). Selected crop factors for Texas include irrigated rice, 1.05; pecan trees, 0.65; corn, 0.80; cotton, 0.65; and grass/lawn, 0.80. To calculate the water need for a lawn in south-central Texas, for example, multiply the PET of 88 inches by a crop factor of 0.80 to give an annual water need of 70.4 inches. To determine the irrigation requirement, subtract the annual precipitation of 35 inches from an annual crop water need of 70.4 inches, which produces an annual irrigation requirement of 35.4 inches or 21.8 gallons per square foot.

Managing Texas' water resources would be much easier if each location could depend on its mean annual precipitation every year. Texas, unfortunately, has among the most variable precipitation regimes in the United States, so large year-to-year swings occur (Goudie and Wilkinson 1977; Norwine, Giardino, and Krishnamurthy 2005). In 2004, for instance, San Marcos had over 52 inches of precipitation, but in the next year the Central Texas city had less than half as much (NCDC 2006). The erratic precipitation regime truly makes Texas a land of floods and droughts. Greater annual swings in precipitation trend westward, so precipitation averages are rarely the normal values for most of the state (Bomar 1995). This year-to-year variability plays havoc with water resource plans and agricultural operations (Legates 2004; Earl, Dixon, and Day 2006). One year of precipitation can provide a bumper crop, and the next year may produce substantially less, as this table emphasizes.

Average Annual Moisture Regimes	Examples of Cities	Average Annual Precipitation/ Moisture Regime/ Agricultural Options	Wet Annual Precipitation/ Moisture Regime/ Agricultural Options	Dry Annual Precipitation/ Moisture Regime/ Agricultural Options
Humid	Houston	50 inches/ humid/ any annual crops	70 inches/superhumid/ any annual crops	35 inches/subhumid/ most annual crops
Subhumid	San Marcos	35 inches/ subhumid/ most annual crops	50 inches/humid/any annual crops	25 inches/semiarid/ small grains (e.g., wheat, sorghum) and grazing
Semiarid	Lubbock	20 inches/semiarid/ small grains (e.g., wheat, sorghum) and grazing	30 inches/subhumid/ most annual crops and grazing	10 inches/arid/ grazing only
Arid	El Paso	10 inches/arid/grazing only	18 inches/semiarid/ good grazing	5 inches/hyperarid/ no crops or grazing

Climates

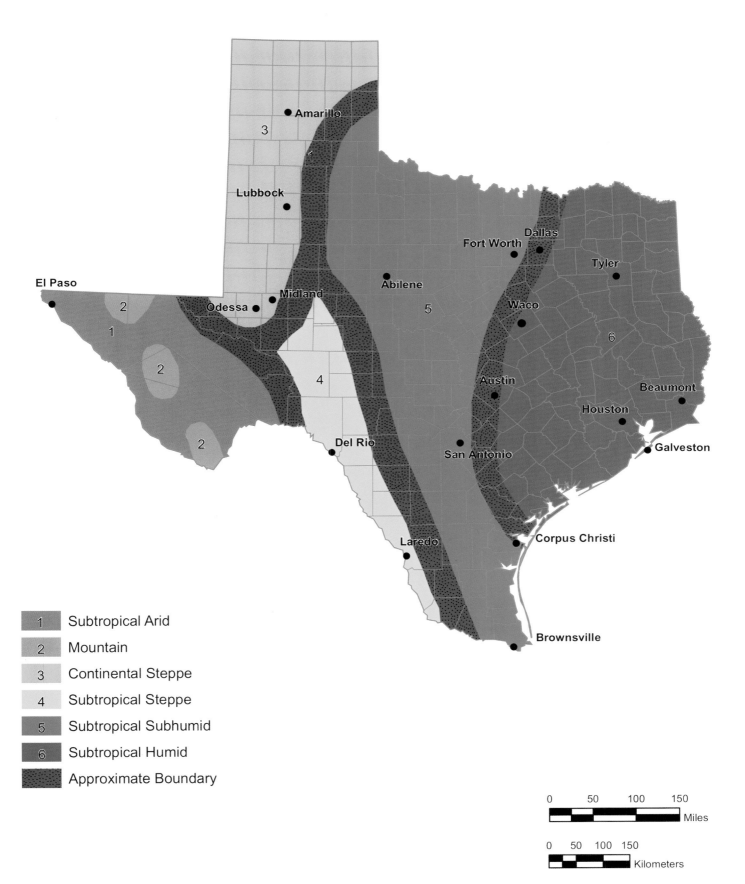

1 Subtropical Arid
2 Mountain
3 Continental Steppe
4 Subtropical Steppe
5 Subtropical Subhumid
6 Subtropical Humid
   Approximate Boundary

0   50   100   150
Miles

0   50   100   150
Kilometers

Source: Larkin and Bomar, 1983.

3

Climate Divisions

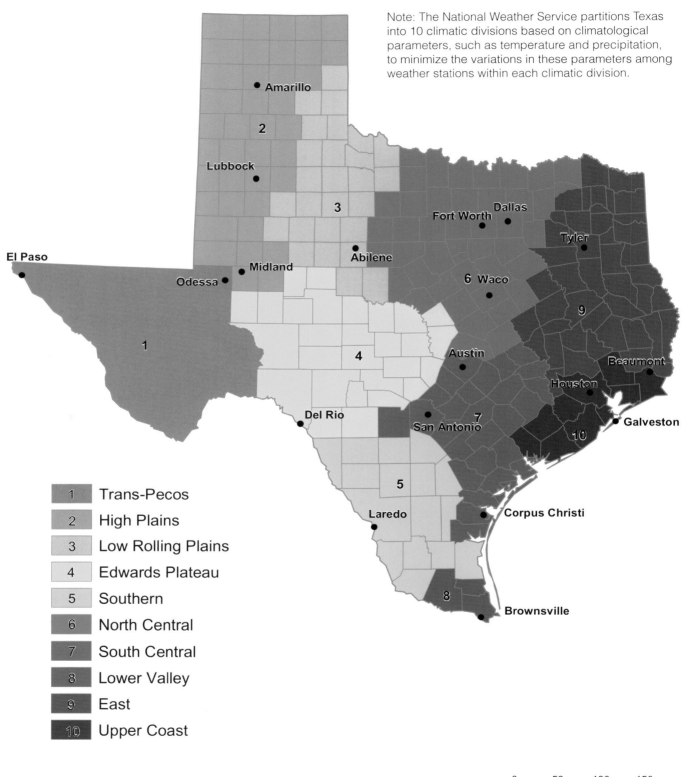

Note: The National Weather Service partitions Texas into 10 climatic divisions based on climatological parameters, such as temperature and precipitation, to minimize the variations in these parameters among weather stations within each climatic division.

1	Trans-Pecos
2	High Plains
3	Low Rolling Plains
4	Edwards Plateau
5	Southern
6	North Central
7	South Central
8	Lower Valley
9	East
10	Upper Coast

Source: National Weather Service, 1959.

Average Annual Precipitation

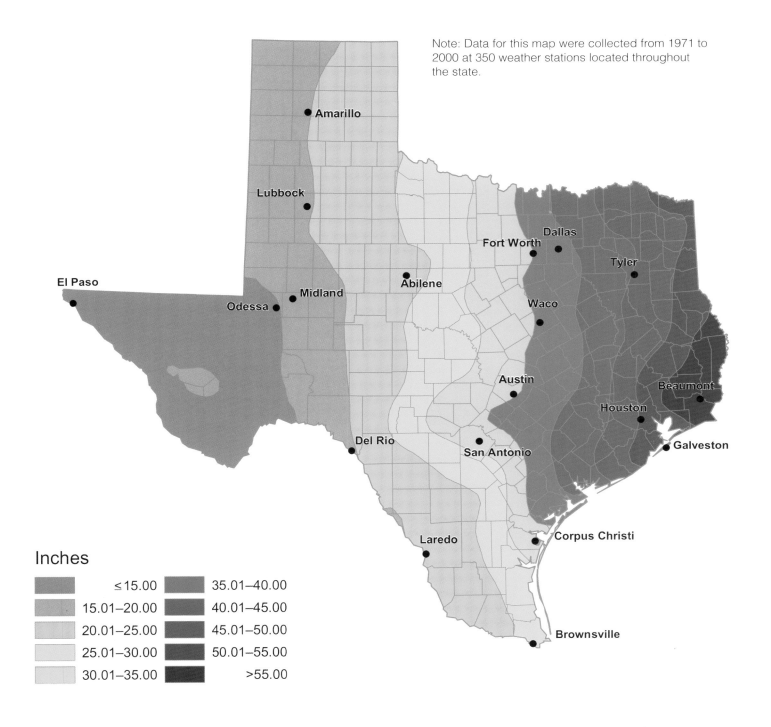

Note: Data for this map were collected from 1971 to 2000 at 350 weather stations located throughout the state.

Inches

≤15.00	35.01–40.00
15.01–20.00	40.01–45.00
20.01–25.00	45.01–50.00
25.01–30.00	50.01–55.00
30.01–35.00	>55.00

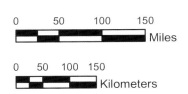

Source: National Oceanographic and Atmospheric Administration, 2002.

Average Monthly Precipitation, January–April

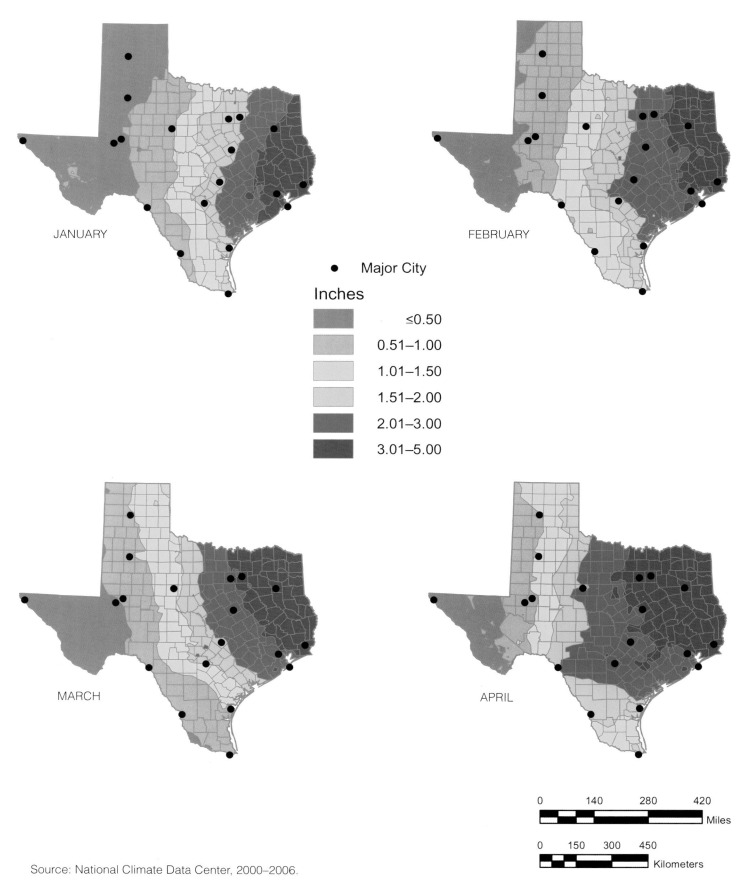

JANUARY

FEBRUARY

MARCH

APRIL

● Major City

Inches

≤0.50

0.51–1.00

1.01–1.50

1.51–2.00

2.01–3.00

3.01–5.00

0   140   280   420
Miles

0   150   300   450
Kilometers

Source: National Climate Data Center, 2000–2006.

Average Monthly Precipitation, May–August

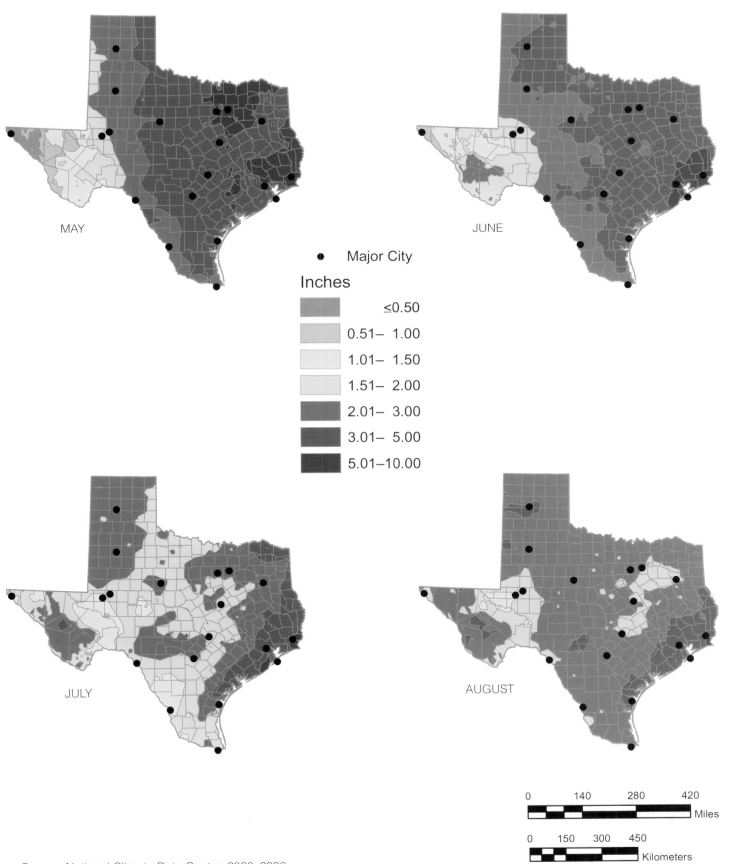

MAY

JUNE

JULY

AUGUST

• Major City

Inches

	≤0.50
	0.51– 1.00
	1.01– 1.50
	1.51– 2.00
	2.01– 3.00
	3.01– 5.00
	5.01–10.00

0   140   280   420
Miles

0   150   300   450
Kilometers

Source: National Climate Data Center, 2000–2006.

Average Monthly Precipitation, September–December

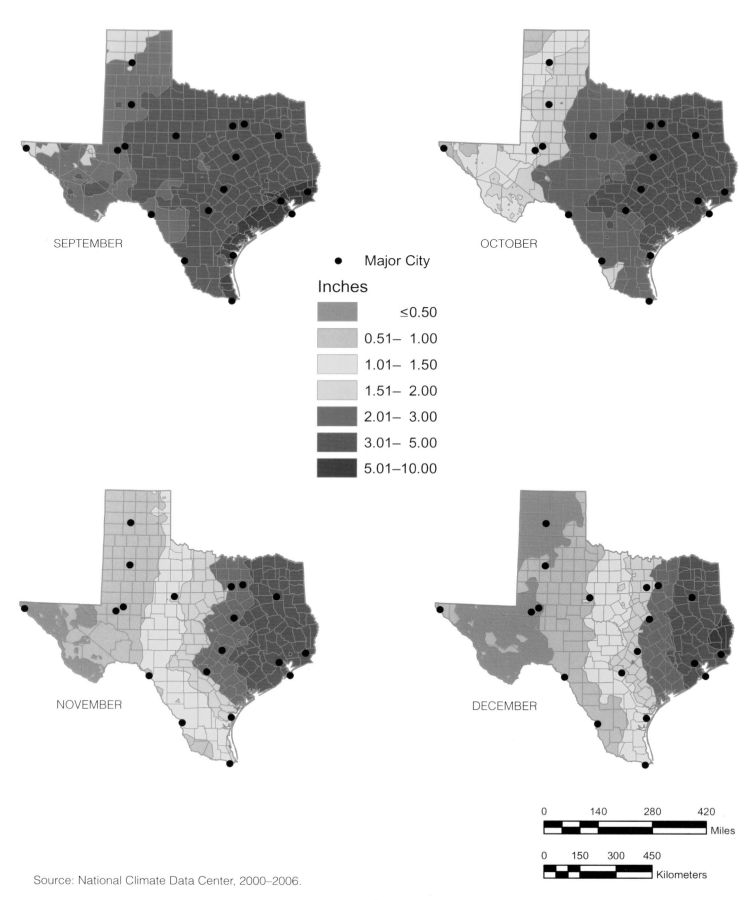

Major City

Inches

	≤0.50
	0.51– 1.00
	1.01– 1.50
	1.51– 2.00
	2.01– 3.00
	3.01– 5.00
	5.01–10.00

SEPTEMBER

OCTOBER

NOVEMBER

DECEMBER

0   140   280   420
Miles

0   150   300   450
Kilometers

Source: National Climate Data Center, 2000–2006.

Climate Variability
Annual Precipitation

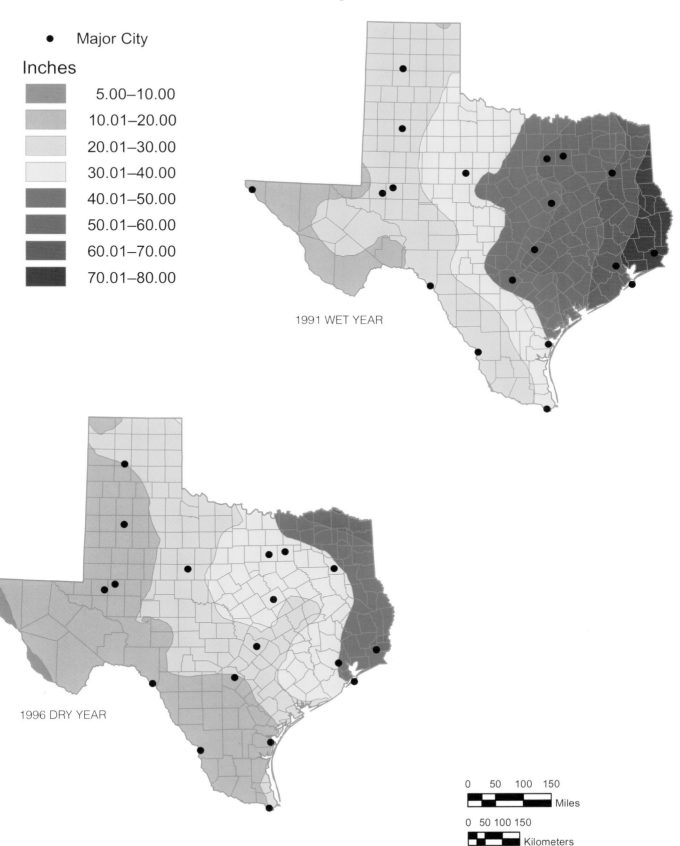

● Major City

Inches

5.00–10.00
10.01–20.00
20.01–30.00
30.01–40.00
40.01–50.00
50.01–60.00
60.01–70.00
70.01–80.00

1991 WET YEAR

1996 DRY YEAR

0 50 100 150 Miles

0 50 100 150 Kilometers

Source: National Climate Data Center, 2004.

Climate Variability
Annual Precipitation

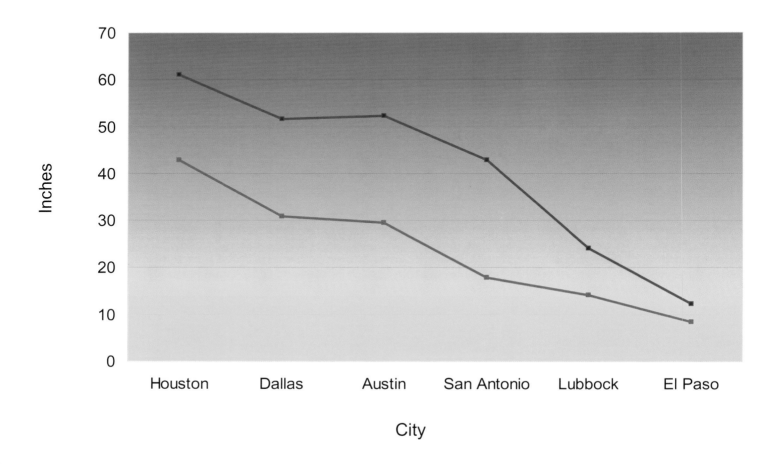

Source: National Climate Data Center, 2005.

Annual Precipitation for Major Texas Cities, 1940–2003

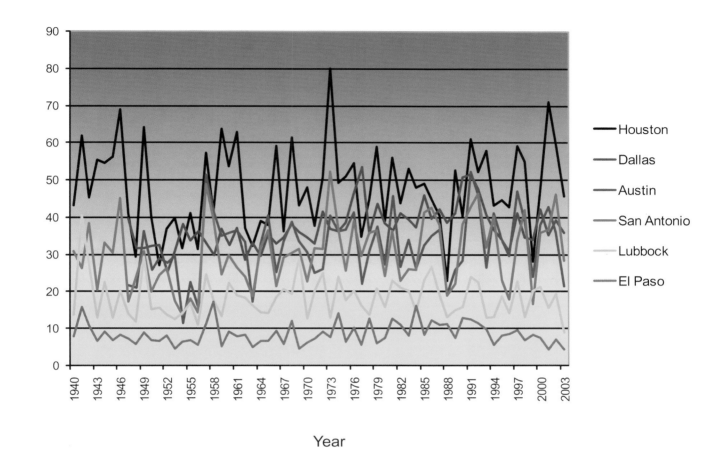

Source: National Climate Data Center, 2005.

Annual Precipitation, 1940–2003
El Paso and Lubbock

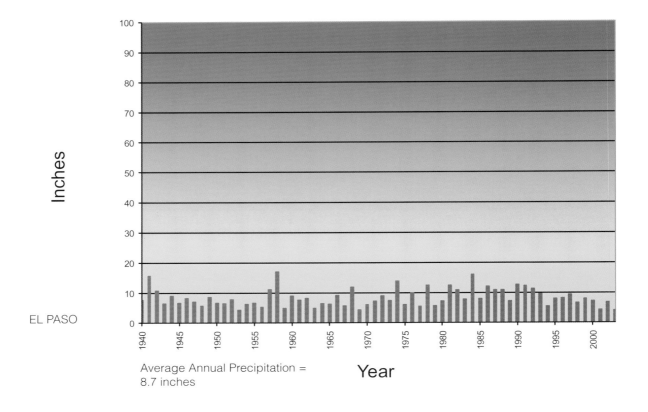

Inches

Year

EL PASO

Average Annual Precipitation =
8.7 inches

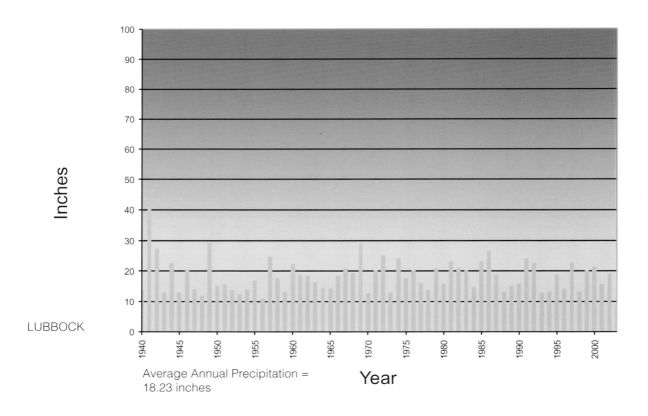

Inches

Year

LUBBOCK

Average Annual Precipitation =
18.23 inches

Source: National Climate Data Center, 2005.

Annual Precipitation, 1940–2003
San Antonio and Austin

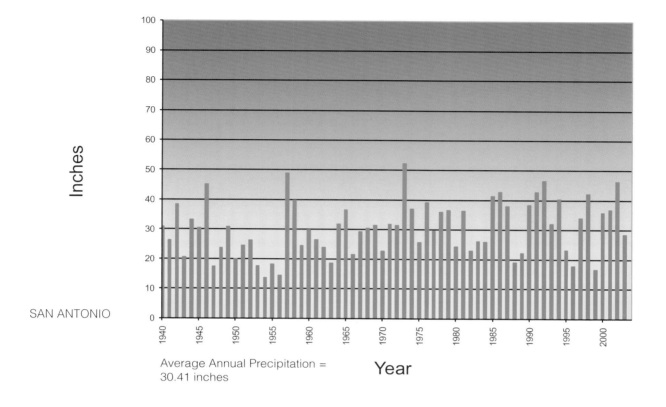

SAN ANTONIO

Average Annual Precipitation =
30.41 inches

Year

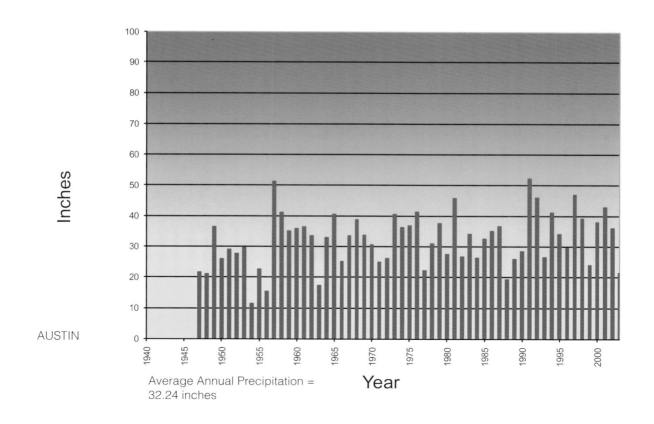

AUSTIN

Average Annual Precipitation =
32.24 inches

Year

Source: National Climate Data Center, 2005.

Annual Precipitation, 1940–2003
Dallas and Houston

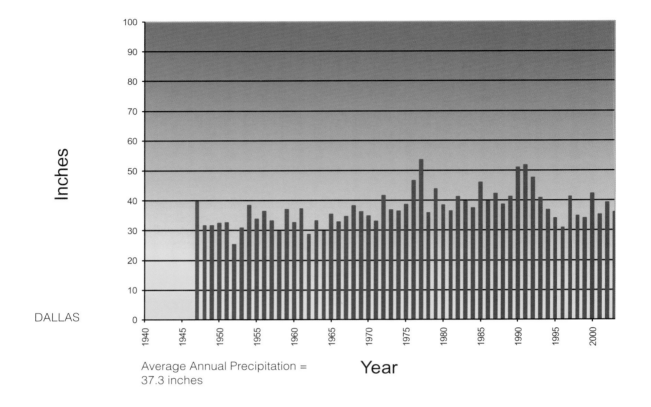

DALLAS

Average Annual Precipitation =
37.3 inches

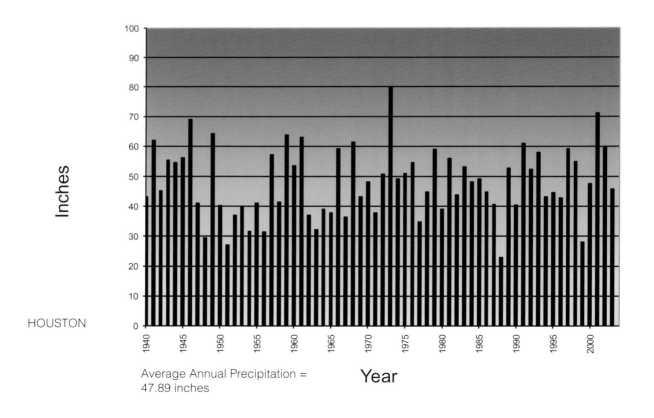

HOUSTON

Average Annual Precipitation =
47.89 inches

Source: National Climate Data Center, 2005.

Annual Potential Evapotranspiration
Priestly Taylor Method

The Priestly Taylor Method measures potential evapotranspiration using soil heat flux and net radiation. The method is an evaluation of how much water is needed to replace the amount that plants are using in an area.

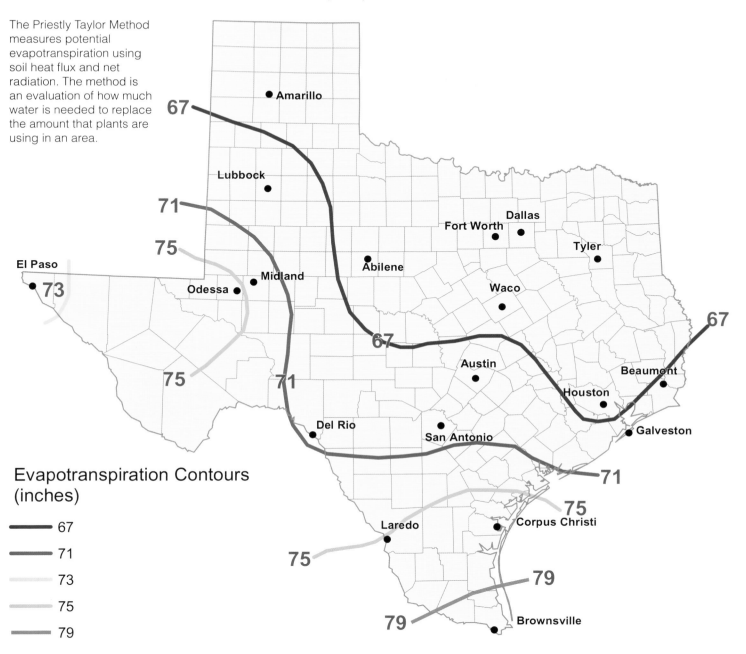

Evapotranspiration Contours (inches)

———	67
———	71
———	73
———	75
———	79

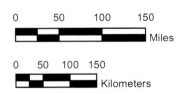

Source: Dugas and Ainsworth, 1983.

Annual Potential Evapotranspiration
Penman Method

The Penman Method, like the Priestly Taylor Method, measures evapotranspiration using soil heat flux and net radiation to calculate the amount of evapotranspiration. However, Penman also includes wind speed through an energy balance equation.

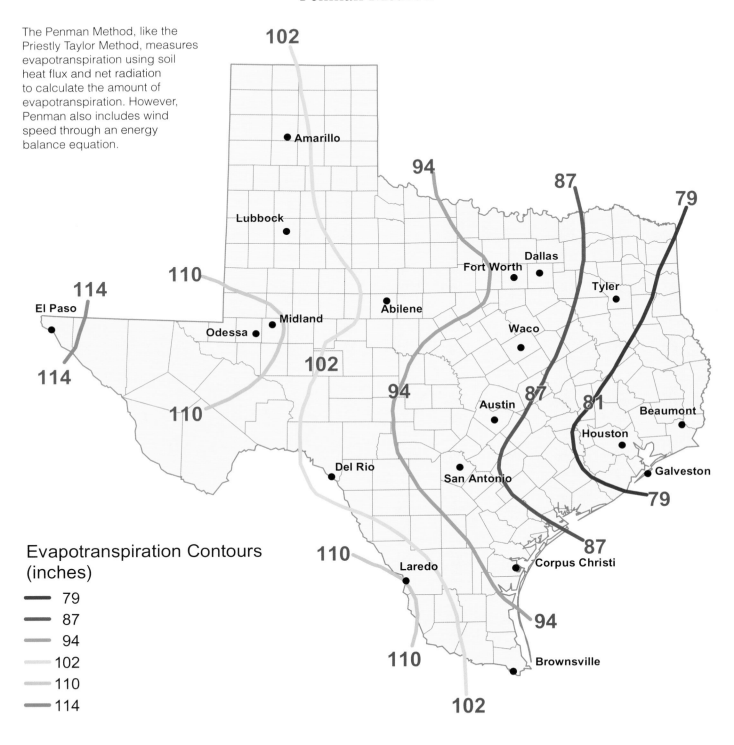

Evapotranspiration Contours (inches)

- —— 79
- —— 87
- —— 94
- —— 102
- —— 110
- —— 114

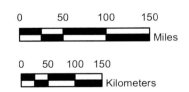

Source: Dugas and Ainsworth, 1983.

Gross Lake Surface Evaporation
Average Annual Rate, 1950–79

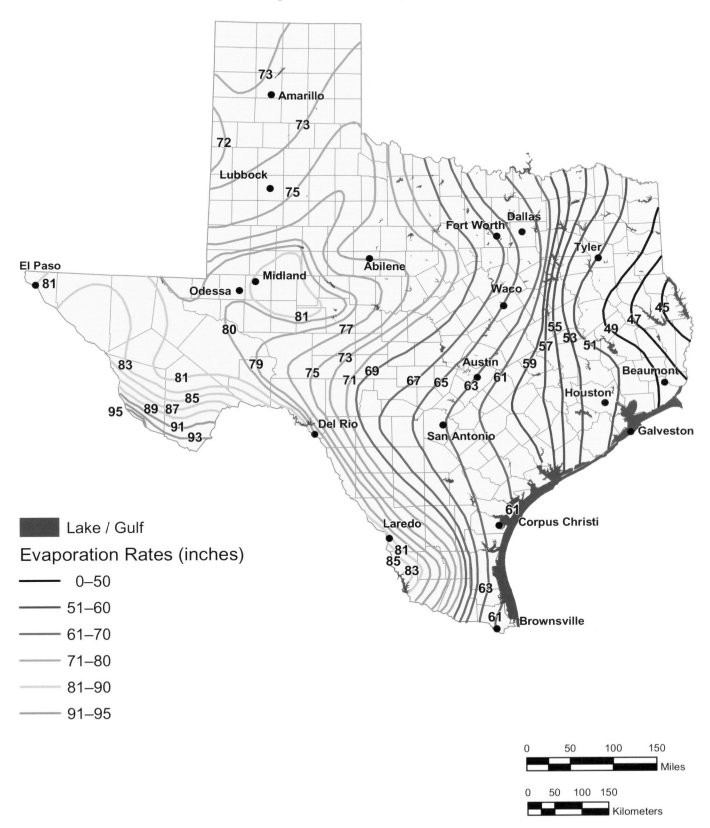

Lake / Gulf

Evaporation Rates (inches)

——	0–50
——	51–60
——	61–70
——	71–80
——	81–90
——	91–95

0   50   100   150
Miles

0   50   100   150
Kilometers

Source: Larkin and Bomar, 1983.

2 Surface Water and Groundwater

UNLIKE MANY STATES, TEXAS IS NOT dominated by one or two river systems—fifteen major river systems meander through the state. Although the Rio Grande forms the nearly 1,000 mile-long southwestern border of the state, the modest flow of the river limits its influence to a narrow band roughly 20 miles wide until its floodplain expands to nearly 50 miles across in the lower Rio Grande Valley. A series of rivers flowing in a radial pattern into the Gulf of Mexico drain the remainder of the state, except the Trans-Pecos, the northern Texas Panhandle, and the Red River Valley. Examples of major streams that follow this radial pattern flowing in a southeasterly direction into the Gulf of Mexico are the Nueces, San Antonio, Guadalupe, Colorado, Brazos, Trinity, Neches, and Sabine. The Canadian River, a tributary of the Arkansas, created its valley by slicing west to east through the northern Texas Panhandle. The Red River defines the Texas-Oklahoma border for more than 200 miles, yet its small northward-flowing tributaries affect only a narrow ribbon in north and northeast Texas (USGS 2001; TWDB 2002).

The thirty-seven hundred named rivers and their tributaries have a total stream length of approximately 80,000 miles and enter the Gulf of Mexico via seven major estuaries to form more than 2 million surface acres of saltwater bays from north to south: Sabine Lake and Sabine-Neches Estuary, Galveston Bay and Trinity-San Jacinto Estuary, Matagorda Bay and Lavaca-Colorado Estuary, San Antonio Bay and Guadalupe Estuary, Aransas Bay and Mission-Aransas Estuary, Corpus Christi Bay and Nueces Estuary, and Baffin Bay and Upper Laguna Madre, each rich biological environments that contain a large percentage of the state's wetlands. Human activities are increasingly impairing Texas surface waters in serious ways (TPWD 2006; TCEQ 2006).

Since the late 1800s, many of Texas' streams have been dammed, creating more than two hundred major reservoirs. Dams were initially built for generation of hydroelectricity, flood control, and the storage of irrigation waters. More recently, these dams and reservoirs have focused on recreation and aesthetics. All of the early hydroelectric dams, such as those on the lower Guadalupe River system, are small, raising the water surface less than 50 feet. Today, more than 1.2 million acres of lakes cover the Texas landscape (TPWD 2006).

Wherever large amounts of water seep into the ground from which the water can eventually be withdrawn, a potential subterranean reservoir is formed. These water-storing strata, or aquifers, provide more than half of all the water consumed in Texas. Most of the state, with the exception of the bedrock mountains of the Trans-Pecos, are underlain by usable amounts of groundwater. Aquifers can be composed of either permeable bedrock or permeable sediments such as sand and gravel. Lining most streams are sedimentary aquifers composed of water-saturated river sediment or alluvium that provides seepage inputs for streams.

Aquifers can be classified in several ways, but it is useful to place Texas' aquifers into three groups. First, unconfined aquifers have water levels directly dependent on recharge and flow to the surface whenever their upper saturated layer, the water table, intersects with the surface. Perhaps the most well-known unconfined aquifer is the Ogallala, which extends north beneath the High Plains from the Texas Panhandle all the way to South Dakota. Second, confined aquifers are saturated layers bounded above and below by largely impervious rocks called aquicludes, which place the contained water under pressure. Confined aquifers, such as those that feed the San Solomon Springs in West Texas, flow under artesian pressure if the confined layer intersects the surface and the water table is sufficiently high. Finally, karst aquifers are contained in limestone and marble rocks that often form "rock sponges" filled with numerous small channels and, in some cases, large underground caverns and "streams." One of the most famous aquifers in the state, the Edwards

Aquifer, is a confined karst aquifer from which water freely discharges from a number of springs along the Balcones Escarpment (Petersen 1995; TWDB 2003; Red River Authority 2004; Edwards Aquifer Authority 2004; Save Our Springs, Inc. 2004).

The amount of water that can be obtained from an aquifer is dependent on both the total capacity of the aquifer—the ability of water to flow through the aquifer, that is, transmissivity—and the rate of recharge. Some aquifers, such as the Edwards, have rapid recharge and high transmissivity and are highly productive provided they receive sufficient recharge. Other aquifers, such as the Ogallala, have immense capacity but negligible recharge. Water from these low-recharge aquifers is, in effect, a nonrenewable resource, and using such water is thus termed "water mining." Once an aquifer like the Ogallala is emptied, it is unlikely to be refilled. Overexploitation of an aquifer can produce subsidence of the overlying surface as sediments settle into voids previously occupied by water. Also, lower water tables often mean more dissolved minerals in the water, making it denser and heavier than purer water. The water at the "bottom of the barrel" has a greater percentage of dissolved solids, as residents of El Paso have discovered with the depletion of the Hueco-Bolson Aquifer (USGS 2005; TWDB 2003; Playa Lakes Joint Venture 2004).

Springs form where saturated aquifers intersect the surface, usually along fault lines where water-bearing rocks have been exposed to the surface. The Balcones Escarpment is a premier location for springs. For a distance of over 300 miles the Miocene-aged (circa 25 million years ago) faulting has broken and exposed the Edwards Limestone so that a number of prolific springs emerge. These springs form the locus of settlement for San Antonio, New Braunfels, San Marcos, Austin, and Georgetown, among other communities along the "spring line" (TWDB 2003; Edwards Aquifer Authority 2004). Also dependent on the flow of some Texas springs are unique biological habitats for a number of endemic and endangered species. Legal protection of these endemics under the federal Endangered Species Act has led to legal action to restrict pumping of aquifers sustaining such springs, most notably the San Antonio section of the Edwards Aquifer.

Natural depressions in the land, periodic floods, and cyclical tides along the coasts create distinctive environments consisting of part water and part land—wetlands. These wetlands, particularly along the coast, are rich environments with a remarkable diversity of plants and animals that make them among the most biologically diverse and productive of all ecosystems. Coastal wetlands are indeed the "nurseries" for many commercially important marine species, such as shrimp, crabs, and redfish. Across the state on the High Plains, wetting and subsequent subsidence of porous sediments have created depressions that are periodically flooded to form "playa lakes," critical habitats for migrating waterfowl. Along Texas rivers, wetlands absorb floodwaters and remove pollutants.

Because of the wetlands' environmental benefits, the federal 1977 Clean Water Act mandated a "No Overall Net Loss" policy for wetlands to protect these fragile environments. This law, combined with the need and desire for wetland habitats for water quality and aesthetic purposes, has led to the creation of numerous "constructed wetlands" across the state. In a 2001 decision, the U.S. Supreme Court ruled that for wetlands to be protected under the No Overall Net Loss policy, they must be hydrologically connected to adjacent federally "navigable" water bodies. Such wetlands are "jurisdictional wetlands" in contrast to those in the U.S. Fish and Wildlife Service Wetlands Inventory, which are protected based on their biological habitats (TWDB 2006; TCEQ 2006; USGS 2006; Texas Water Law Institute 1997; U.S. Federal Highway Administration 2001).

Major Rivers

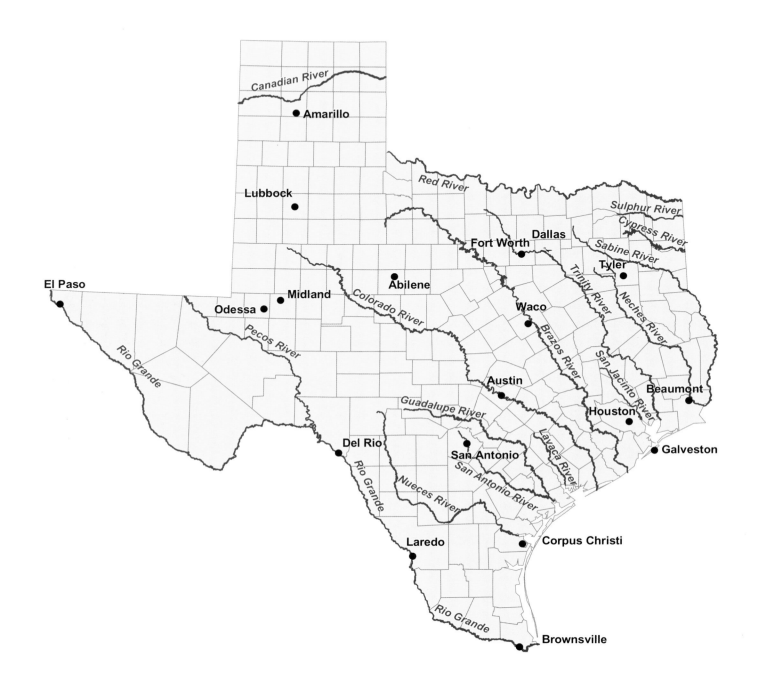

Canadian River

● Amarillo

Red River

Lubbock

Sulphur River

Cypress River

Dallas

Fort Worth

Sabine River

Tyler

El Paso

Abilene

Colorado River

Waco

Trinity River

Neches River

Midland

Odessa

Pecos River

Brazos River

Rio Grande

San Jacinto River

Austin

Beaumont

Guadalupe River

Houston

San Antonio

Lavaca River

Galveston

Del Rio

Rio Grande

Nueces River

San Antonio River

Laredo

Corpus Christi

Rio Grande

Brownsville

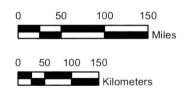

0   50   100   150
Miles

0   50   100   150
Kilometers

Sources: U.S. Geological Survey, 2001; Environmental Systems Research Institute, 2002.

Major Drainage Basins

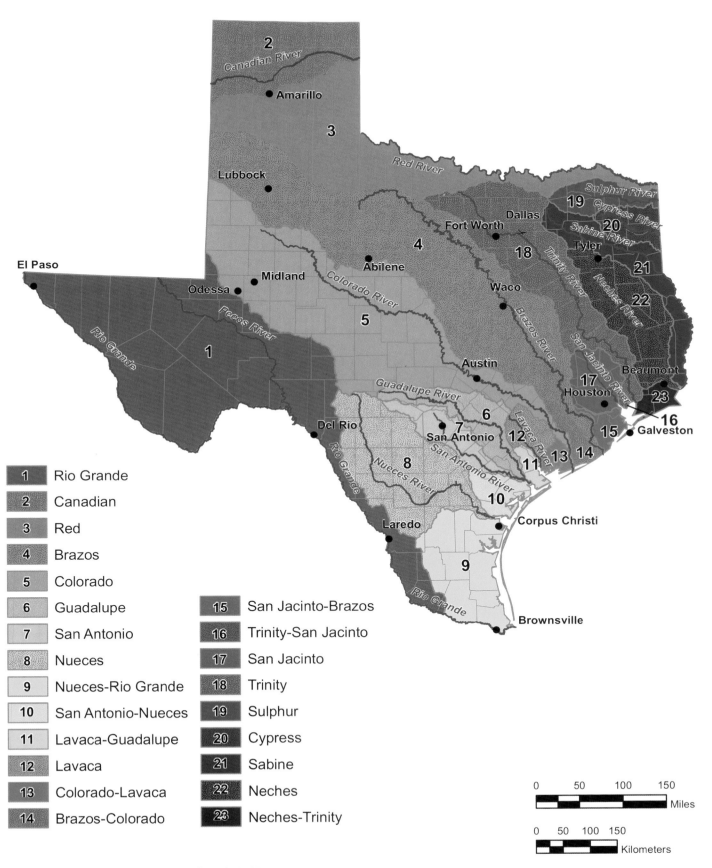

1	Rio Grande
2	Canadian
3	Red
4	Brazos
5	Colorado
6	Guadalupe
7	San Antonio
8	Nueces
9	Nueces-Rio Grande
10	San Antonio-Nueces
11	Lavaca-Guadalupe
12	Lavaca
13	Colorado-Lavaca
14	Brazos-Colorado
15	San Jacinto-Brazos
16	Trinity-San Jacinto
17	San Jacinto
18	Trinity
19	Sulphur
20	Cypress
21	Sabine
22	Neches
23	Neches-Trinity

Source: Texas Water Development Board, 2002.

Surface Water

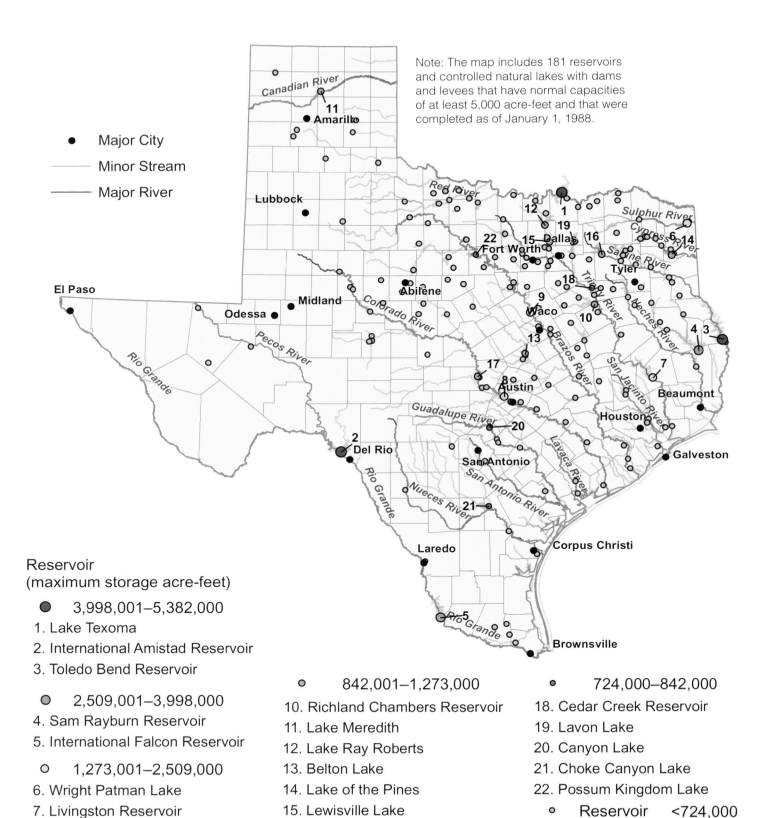

Note: The map includes 181 reservoirs and controlled natural lakes with dams and levees that have normal capacities of at least 5,000 acre-feet and that were completed as of January 1, 1988.

- ● Major City
- ⎯ Minor Stream
- ⎯ Major River

Reservoir
(maximum storage acre-feet)

● 3,998,001–5,382,000
1. Lake Texoma
2. International Amistad Reservoir
3. Toledo Bend Reservoir

● 2,509,001–3,998,000
4. Sam Rayburn Reservoir
5. International Falcon Reservoir

○ 1,273,001–2,509,000
6. Wright Patman Lake
7. Livingston Reservoir
8. Lake Travis
9. Whitney Reservoir

○ 842,001–1,273,000
10. Richland Chambers Reservoir
11. Lake Meredith
12. Lake Ray Roberts
13. Belton Lake
14. Lake of the Pines
15. Lewisville Lake
16. Lake Tawakoni
17. Lake Buchanan

○ 724,000–842,000
18. Cedar Creek Reservoir
19. Lavon Lake
20. Canyon Lake
21. Choke Canyon Lake
22. Possum Kingdom Lake

○ Reservoir   <724,000

| 0 | 50 | 100 | 150 |
Miles

| 0 | 50 | 100 | 150 |
Kilometers

Source: U.S. Geological Survey, 2001.

2.4. MAJOR TEXAS RESERVOIRS

Order by maximum storage	Name	River	Drainage Area (sq. mi.)	Total Maximum Storage Acre-Feet/ Elevation in Feet	Conservation Storage Acre-Feet/ Elevation in Feet	Builder/Operator
1	Lake Texoma	Red	39,719	5,382,000/640	2,643,000/ 617	U.S. Army Corps of Engineers
2	International Amistad Reservoir	Rio Grande	123,143	5,250,000/1,140	3,505,000/ 1,117	U.S. Bureau of Reclamation/International Boundary and Water Commission
3	Toledo Bend Reservoir	Sabine	7,178	4,661,000/173	4,472,000/172	Sabine River Authority
4	Sam Rayburn Reservoir	Neches	3,349	3,998,000/176	2,898,000/164	U.S. Army Corps of Engineers
5	International Falcon Reservoir	Rio Grande	159,270	3,280,700/307	2,767,000/301	U.S. Bureau of Reclamation/International Boundary and Water Commission
6	Wright Patman Lake	Sulphur	3,400	2,509,000/259	145,000/220	U.S. Army Corps of Engineers
7	Livingston Reservoir	Trinity	16,580	2,150,000/135	1,750,000/131	Trinity River Authority
8	Lake Travis	Colorado	approx. 39,000	1,954,000/714	1,173.000/681	Lower Colorado River Authority
9	Whitney Reservoir	Brazos	27,190	1,620,000/571	379,000/520	U.S. Army Corps of Engineers
10	Richland Chambers	Trinity	1,960	1,273,000/317	1,136,000/314	Trinity River Authority
11	Lake Meredith	Canadian	20,220	1,098,000/3,004	780,000/2,935	U.S. Bureau of Reclamation/Canadian River Municipal Authority
12	Lake Ray Roberts	Trinity	692	1,064,000	800,000/633	U.S. Army Corps of Engineers
13	Belton Lake	Leon	3,531	1,086,000	442,000/594	U.S. Army Corps of Engineers
14	Lake of the Pines	Cypress	850	982,000/250	252,000/228	U.S. Army Corps of Engineers
15	Lewisville Lake	Trinity	1,660	981,000/532	640,000/515	U.S. Army Corps of Engineers
16	Lake Tawakoni	Sabine	756	926,000	888,000/438	Sabine River Authority
17	Lake Buchanan	Colorado	approx. 32,000	922,000/1,021	875,600/1,020	Lower Colorado River Authority
18	Cedar Creek Reservoir	Cedar Creek	1,007	842,000/325	637,000/322	Tarrant County Water Control District
19	Lavon Lake	Trinity	770	748,000/504	444,000/491	U.S. Army Corps of Engineers
20	Canyon Lake	Guadalupe	1,430	740,000/943	337,000/909	U.S. Army Corps of Engineers
21	Choke Canyon Lake	Frio	5,490	731,000/222	695,000/220	City of Corpus Christi
22	Possum Kingdom Lake	Brazos	23,600	724,000/1,001	556,000/1,000	Brazos River Authority

Sources: U.S. Geological Survey, 2005; listed water resource agencies, 2005.

Note: When specific values are not provided, values are calculated from stage and volume relationships.

Springs

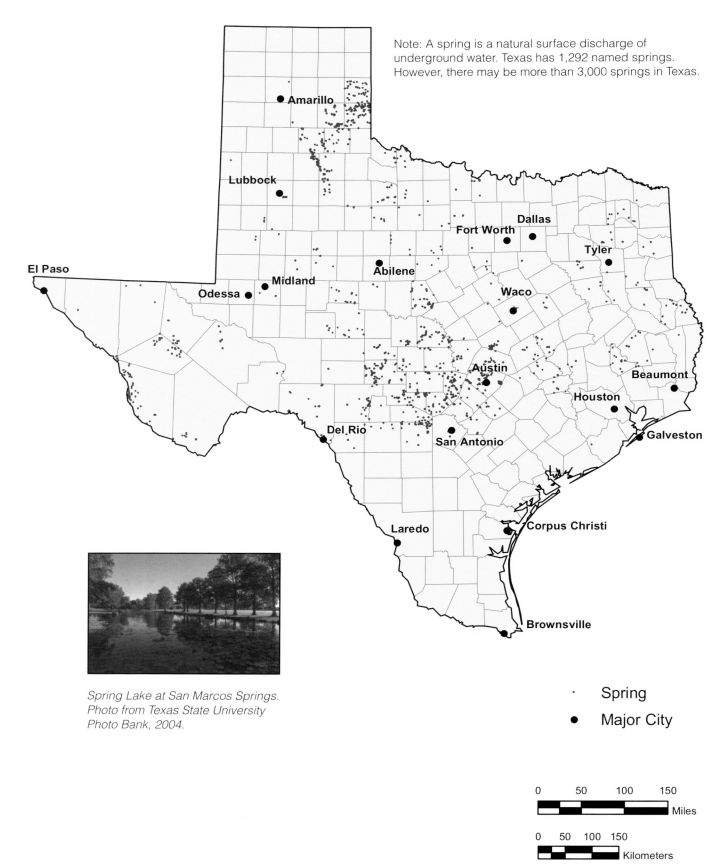

Note: A spring is a natural surface discharge of underground water. Texas has 1,292 named springs. However, there may be more than 3,000 springs in Texas.

Spring Lake at San Marcos Springs. Photo from Texas State University Photo Bank, 2004.

·   Spring

●   Major City

0   50   100   150
Miles

0   50   100   150
Kilometers

Source: Texas Water Development Board, 2004; Besse, 2007.

Groundwater Recharge
Estimated Mean Annual

Note: The estimated mean annual natural groundwater recharge data set was generated by multiplying a grid of mean annual runoff values by a grid of base-flow index values that are assumed to represent reasonably the long-term percentage of natural groundwater discharge in stream flow. Further assumed was that the long-term average natural groundwater recharge is equal to long-term average natural groundwater discharge to streams.

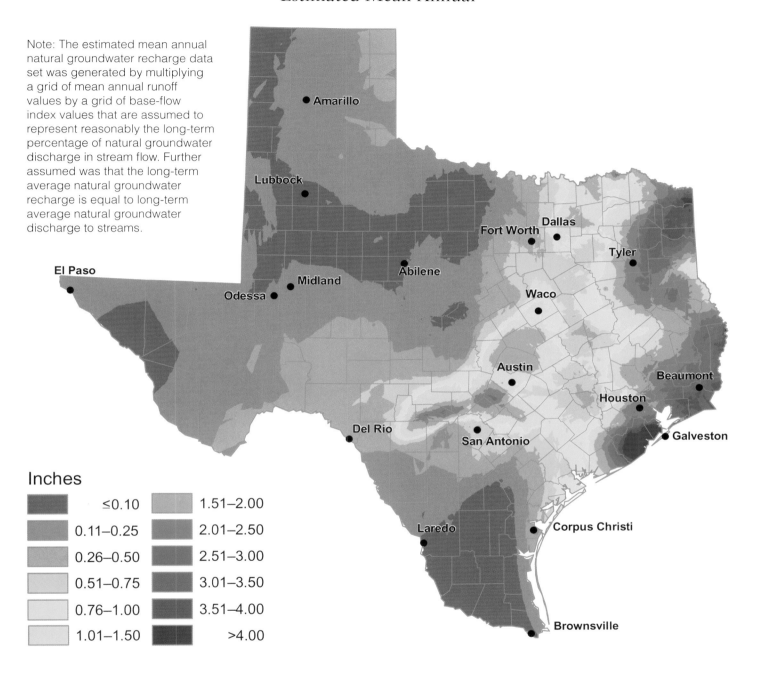

Inches

≤0.10	1.51–2.00
0.11–0.25	2.01–2.50
0.26–0.50	2.51–3.00
0.51–0.75	3.01–3.50
0.76–1.00	3.51–4.00
1.01–1.50	>4.00

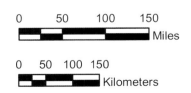

Major Aquifers

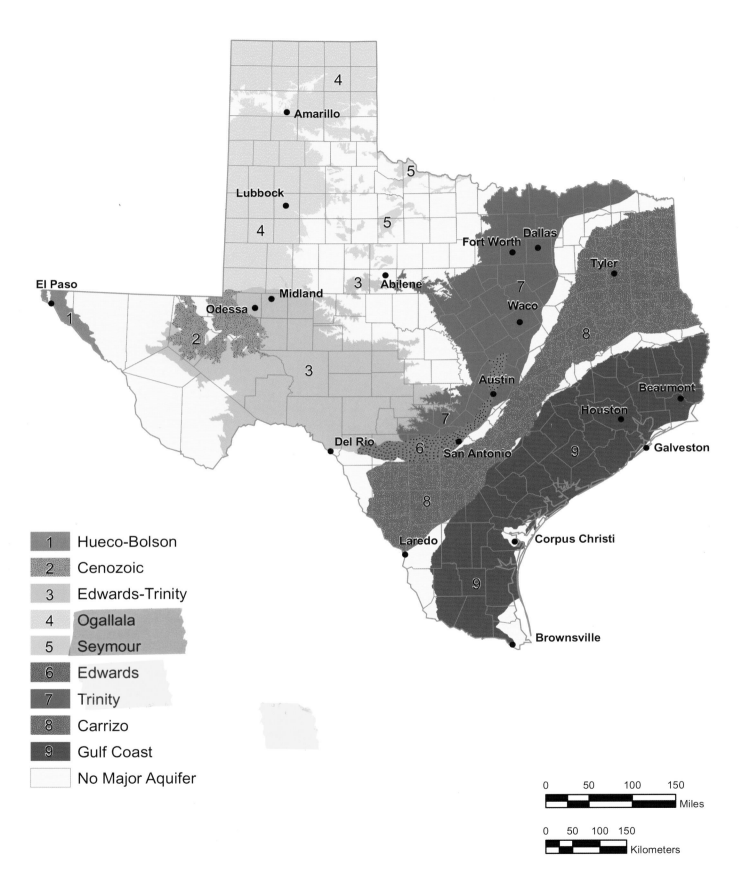

1 Hueco-Bolson
2 Cenozoic
3 Edwards-Trinity
4 Ogallala
5 Seymour
6 Edwards
7 Trinity
8 Carrizo
9 Gulf Coast
No Major Aquifer

0   50   100   150
Miles

0   50   100   150
Kilometers

Source: Texas Water Development Board, 2003.

26

Edwards Aquifer

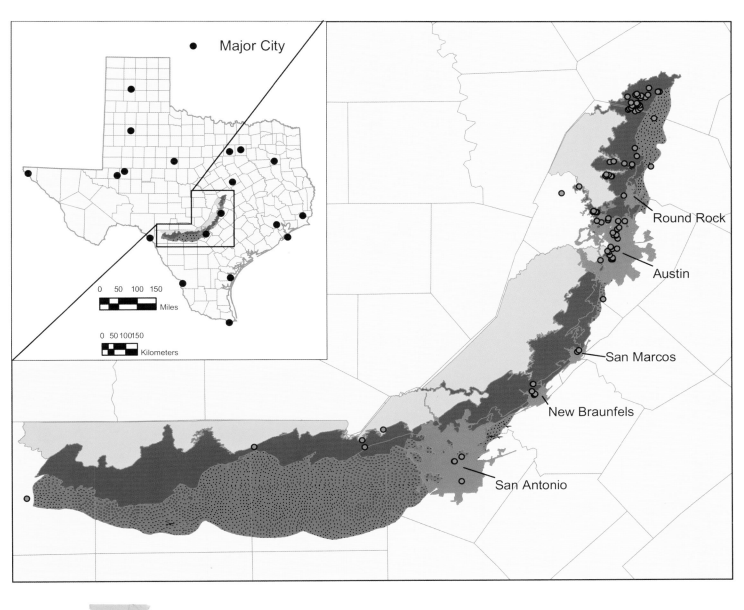

Major City

Round Rock

Austin

San Marcos

New Braunfels

San Antonio

Edwards Aquifer

Contributing Zone
Recharge Zone
Artesian Zone

City Population

● 10,001–20,000

▬ >20,000

○ Edwards Aquifer Spring

0 10 20 30 Miles

0 10 20 30 Kilometers

0 50 100 150 Miles

0 50 100 150 Kilometers

The Edwards Aquifer is one of the greatest natural resources in Texas, providing water for almost 2 million people in south-central Texas. Because demand for its water is increasing rapidly, water users in the area face decisions about who owns, controls, and uses the water from the Edwards Aquifer.

Source: Texas Water Development Board, 2003; The Edwards Aquifer Authority, 2004.

Ogallala Aquifer

The Ogallala Aquifer underlies approximately 225,000 square miles of the Great Plains and extends 800 miles north to south and 400 miles east to west. The aquifer underlies parts of Colorado, Kansas, Nebraska, New Mexico, Oklahoma, South Dakota, Texas, and Wyoming. The depth to water below land surface ranges between 100 and 400 feet. The groundwater is fresh with some calcium, magnesium, and bicarbonate. The Rocky Mountains were originally the aquifer's natural recharging source. However, the Rockies have not supplied the aquifer for more than 10,000 years. A lack of rainfall, large rivers below the aquifer's water table, over-irrigation, and low-porosity material prevent the aquifer from recharging adequately. The level of the aquifer is declining at an estimated 1.74 feet per year.

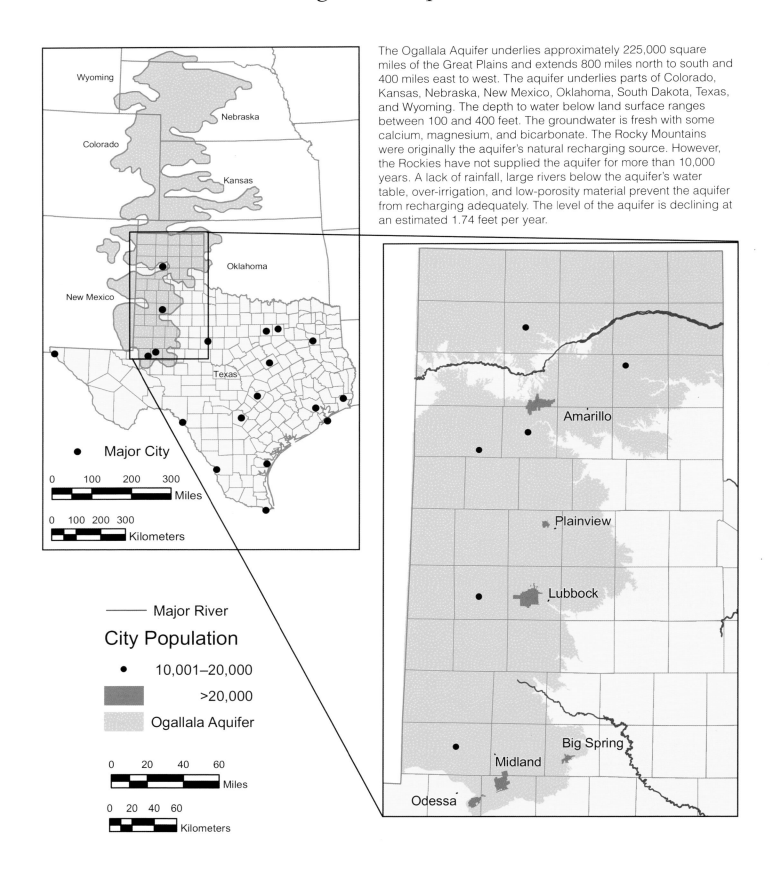

Major City

0   100   200   300
Miles

0   100 200 300
Kilometers

Major River

City Population

● 10,001–20,000

▬ >20,000

▢ Ogallala Aquifer

0   20   40   60
Miles

0   20 40 60
Kilometers

Sources: Texas Water Development Board, 2003; Red River Authority of Texas, 2004.

Edwards-Trinity Aquifer System

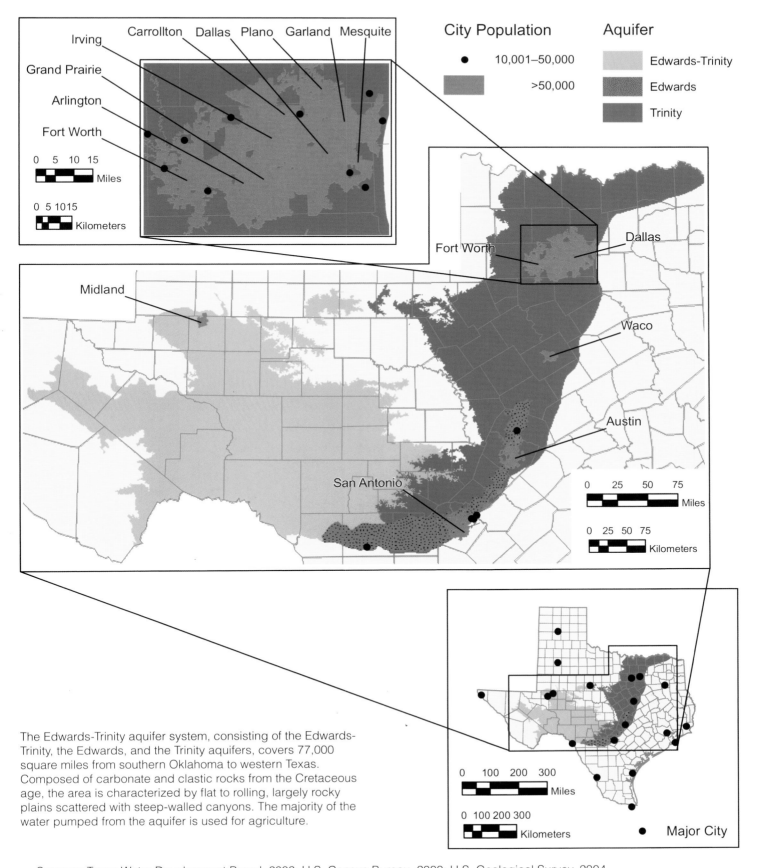

City Population

- 10,001–50,000
- >50,000

Aquifer

- Edwards-Trinity
- Edwards
- Trinity

Irving
Carrollton Dallas Plano Garland Mesquite
Grand Prairie
Arlington
Fort Worth

0 5 10 15 Miles
0 5 10 15 Kilometers

Fort Worth   Dallas

Midland
Waco
Austin
San Antonio

0 25 50 75 Miles
0 25 50 75 Kilometers

The Edwards-Trinity aquifer system, consisting of the Edwards-Trinity, the Edwards, and the Trinity aquifers, covers 77,000 square miles from southern Oklahoma to western Texas. Composed of carbonate and clastic rocks from the Cretaceous age, the area is characterized by flat to rolling, largely rocky plains scattered with steep-walled canyons. The majority of the water pumped from the aquifer is used for agriculture.

0 100 200 300 Miles
0 100 200 300 Kilometers

• Major City

Sources: Texas Water Development Board, 2003; U.S. Census Bureau, 2000; U.S. Geological Survey, 2004.

Minor Aquifers

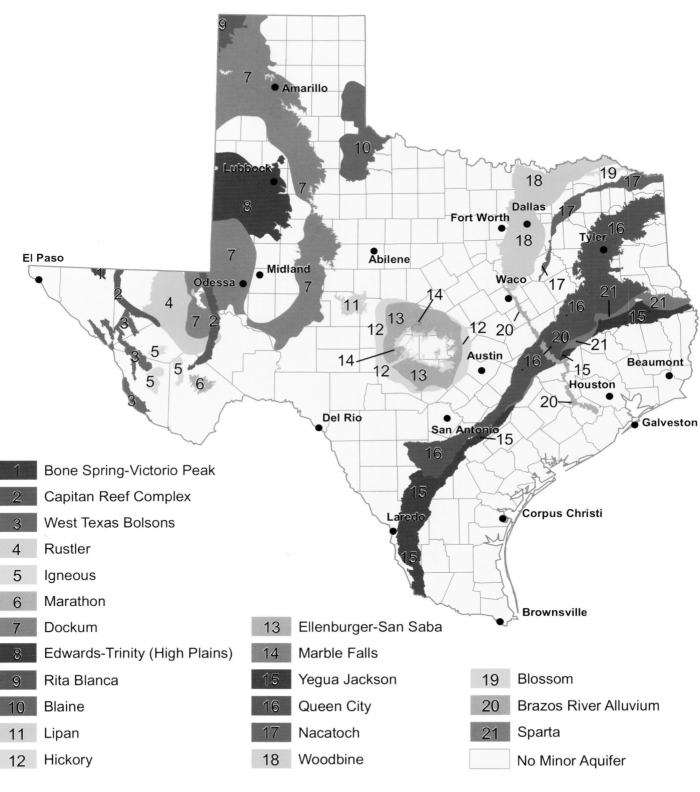

1	Bone Spring-Victorio Peak
2	Capitan Reef Complex
3	West Texas Bolsons
4	Rustler
5	Igneous
6	Marathon
7	Dockum
8	Edwards-Trinity (High Plains)
9	Rita Blanca
10	Blaine
11	Lipan
12	Hickory
13	Ellenburger-San Saba
14	Marble Falls
15	Yegua Jackson
16	Queen City
17	Nacatoch
18	Woodbine
19	Blossom
20	Brazos River Alluvium
21	Sparta
	No Minor Aquifer

Source: Texas Water Development Board, 2003.

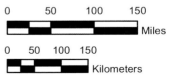

Playa Lakes

Playas are shallow lakes without surface outlets. In Texas, they average 17 acres in size and are round and shallow. These basins hold water from precipitation and, despite being lined with clay, are porous enough to serve as a source of recharge for the Ogallala Aquifer. These unique wetland environments support a diversity of plants, mammals, birds, amphibians, and aquatic invertebrates.

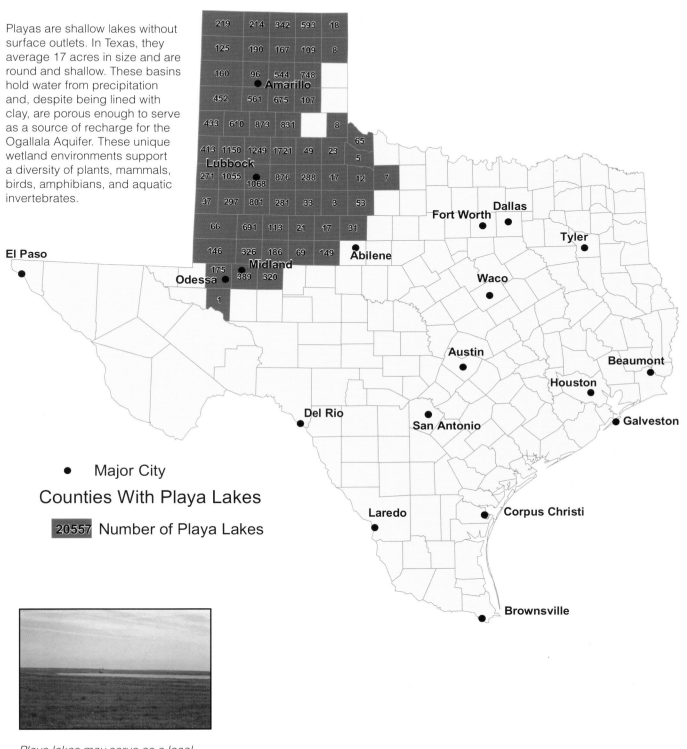

- Major City

Counties With Playa Lakes

20557 Number of Playa Lakes

Playa lakes may serve as a local irrigation water supply source. Photo by U.S. Geological Survey, 2005.

Sources: Fish et al., 2000; Playa Lakes Joint Venture, 2004; U.S. Environmental Protection Agency, 2003.

Coastal Wetlands near Galveston

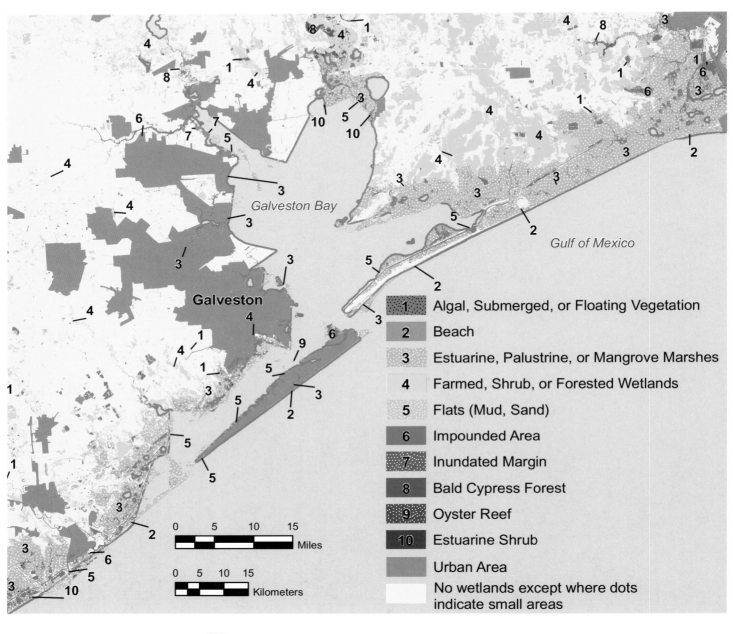

Galveston Bay

Gulf of Mexico

Galveston

1	Algal, Submerged, or Floating Vegetation
2	Beach
3	Estuarine, Palustrine, or Mangrove Marshes
4	Farmed, Shrub, or Forested Wetlands
5	Flats (Mud, Sand)
6	Impounded Area
7	Inundated Margin
8	Bald Cypress Forest
9	Oyster Reef
10	Estuarine Shrub
	Urban Area
	No wetlands except where dots indicate small areas

0   5   10   15   Miles

0   5   10   15   Kilometers

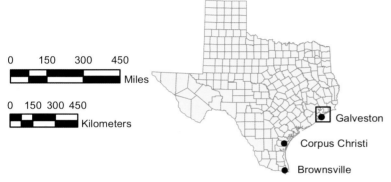

0   150   300   450   Miles

0   150   300   450   Kilometers

Galveston

Corpus Christi

Brownsville

Galveston Bay is the habitat for many forms of wildlife. Photo by Texas Parks and Wildlife Department, 2004.

Source: National Wetlands Inventory, 1992.

Coastal Wetlands near Corpus Christi

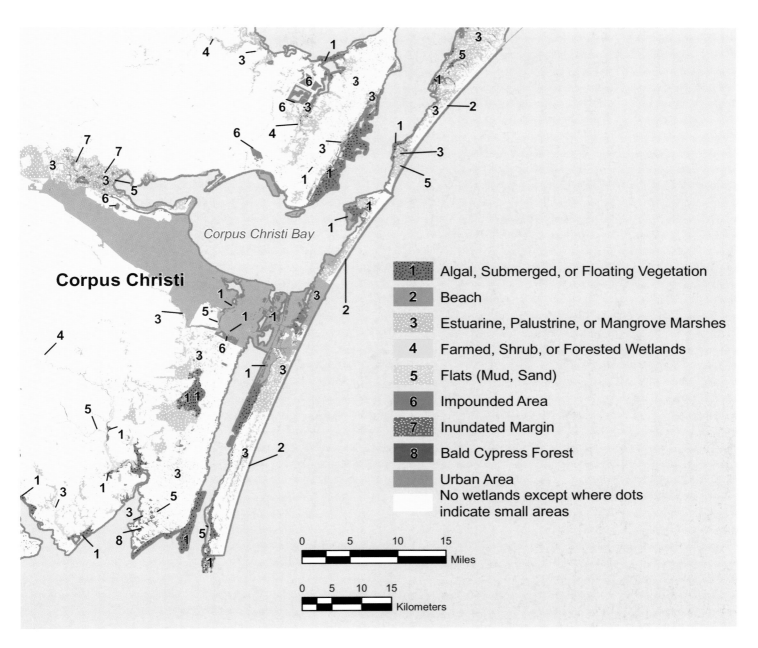

Legend:

- **1** Algal, Submerged, or Floating Vegetation
- **2** Beach
- **3** Estuarine, Palustrine, or Mangrove Marshes
- **4** Farmed, Shrub, or Forested Wetlands
- **5** Flats (Mud, Sand)
- **6** Impounded Area
- **7** Inundated Margin
- **8** Bald Cypress Forest

Urban Area

No wetlands except where dots indicate small areas

Corpus Christi Bay

Corpus Christi

0   5   10   15 Miles

0   5   10   15 Kilometers

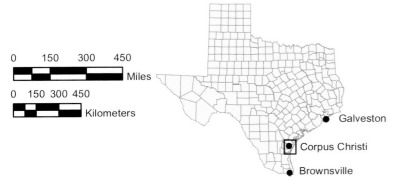

0   150   300   450 Miles

0   150   300   450 Kilometers

Galveston

Corpus Christi

Brownsville

Jetty fishing is a popular sport in Corpus Christi. Photo by Texas Parks and Wildlife Department, 2004.

Source: National Wetlands Inventory, 1992.

Coastal Wetlands near Brownsville

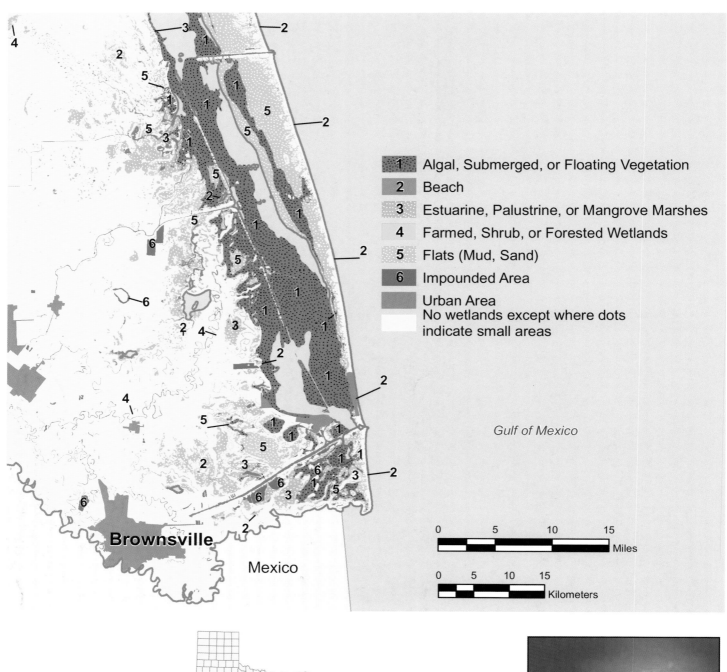

Legend:

1	Algal, Submerged, or Floating Vegetation
2	Beach
3	Estuarine, Palustrine, or Mangrove Marshes
4	Farmed, Shrub, or Forested Wetlands
5	Flats (Mud, Sand)
6	Impounded Area
	Urban Area
	No wetlands except where dots indicate small areas

Gulf of Mexico

Brownsville

Mexico

0   5   10   15 Miles

0   5   10   15 Kilometers

0   150   300   450 Miles

0   150 300 450 Kilometers

Galveston

Corpus Christi

Brownsville

South Texas is known for its sandy beaches. Photo by Texas Parks and Wildlife Department, 2004.

Source: National Wetlands Inventory, 1992.

3 Water Hazards

TEXAS HAS A VARIETY OF NATURAL HAZ-ards that affect human beings in serious ways: floods, droughts, hurricanes, tornadoes, grass and forest fires, erosion, land subsidence, and pestilence. The natural hazards in which water is the focus wreak by far the most damage to humans and our built landscape.

Texas has nearly 6,000 square miles of coastal land that is less than 11.5 feet in elevation, the fourth-largest lowland area in the United States after Louisiana, Florida, and North Carolina. The Texas coastline is a vulnerable area affected by rising sea levels and accompanying tidal action, storm surges and waves, and subsiding land on the state's upper northeastern coast. Rising sea levels caused by worldwide eustasy from melting glaciers, thermal expansion of warming ocean water, and regional subsidence in the northern Gulf of Mexico are almost imperceptible forces that will inextricably continue to accelerate erosion of Texas coastal lands. Large hurricanes are catalysts to this coastal erosion as they drive storm surges and waves that can in just a few days dramatically change sections of the shoreline through scouring, battering, and flooding. Human activities and shoreline structures on the Texas coast, such as dredging, sand mining, groins, and jetties, and projects of a regional scope, including dams and irrigation, exacerbate the loss of coastal land. The three zones of greatest shoreline erosion in Texas are, from north to south, (1) west of Sabine Pass, (2) midway between Galveston Bay and Matagorda Bay, and (3) South Padre Island. The federal and state governments have taken statutory actions to try to mitigate the loss of coastal land and to remove buildings from these threatened areas before storms cause loss of life (Titus and Richman 2001; Mathewson 2006; USGS 2001; EPA 2006; NWS 2006).

Texas floods are notorious. So common and dangerous are Texas floods that popular literature and music are replete with depictions of the threats, deaths, and anguish caused by the raging water. Some of the world's highest-maximum-precipitation events have occurred in Texas; for example, in New Braunfels (16 inches in 4 hours, 1972), Medina (48 inches in 12 hours, 1978), Alvin (43 inches in 24 hours, 1979), and Odem (25 inches in 3.5 hours, 1984). These high-intensity rains cause streams to quickly become powerful torrents of water. From 1853 to 2002, some 256 major or catastrophic storms or floods inundated Texas. In terms of precipitation amounts, the largest flood occurred when 48 inches of rain poured down during August 1–4, 1978, in Shackelford County on the Guadalupe River northwest of San Antonio. The next year, Brazoria County, south of Houston, received 43 inches on July 24–28. On June 6–9, 2001, Houston itself was flooded severely with 36 inches of rain (NWS 2006).

Few places in the state are safe from these destructive floods. In fact, the Balcones Escarpment is known as the "flash flood alley" of North America, as recurrent deluges rush down from the Texas Hill Country onto the Blackland Prairie and cause great havoc in very short periods of time. Other areas of the state, especially those with expansive impervious surfaces, also frequently experience flash floods. The Texas coast is often flooded as hurricanes hit shore and thrust inland with torrential rains. On an annual basis, Texas leads the nation in deaths and property damage caused by floods (USGS 2002, 2006; NWS 2000; TCEQ 2006; USACE 2006; Slade and Patton 2003; Leopold, Wolman, and Miller 1964; Flood Safety 2006).

Floodplains, especially those in East and Central Texas, do not spare the state's large metropolitan centers of Houston, Dallas–Fort Worth, San Antonio, and Austin, where high-density populations and structures are threatened. From 1853 to 2002, Houston, Dallas, Austin, and Brownsville, with flood-prone streams and extensive impervious surfaces, recorded the greatest number of major floods of any places in the state. The Texas coast and its tidal streams, however, compose the largest area of floodplains in the state. Almost annually, hurricane and other tropical storm waves and high-intensity rains wreak devastation across wide swaths of coastal floodplains, causing loss of life and substantial property damage. Tropical Storm Allison, for instance, caused the costly Houston flood of June 2001.

The "Great Galveston Hurricane of 1900," probably a Category 4 storm (winds 131 to 155 miles per hour), killed more people—estimates range from 6,000 to 8,000—than any other single natural disaster in U.S. history. In the past half century, no place on the Texas coast has escaped the wrath of a major hurricane, because broad areas beyond a hurricane's central eye, particularly on the right side of the storms, are affected as a storm makes landfall and pushes inland. In September 1967, Hurricane Beulah, the only Category 4 hurricane in the past fifty years, made landfall in a rural area just northeast of Brownsville and caused 18 deaths and about $100 million in property damage. Three hurricanes have been recorded as Category 3 (winds 111 to 130 miles per hour) when they came ashore in Texas: (1) Audrey, which hit the lower Sabine River Valley in 1957, concentrated its strongest force in Louisiana; (2) Carla, which struck between Matagorda and San Antonio bays in 1961, killed 43 people and caused $300 million in property damage; and (3) Rita, which slammed into the lower Sabine River Valley in 2005, caused 120 deaths and about $10 billion in damage (USGS 2002, 2006; NWS 2000; NOAA 2005; TCEQ 2006; USACE 2006).

Gulf of Mexico hurricanes, on the other hand, can produce useful supplements to regional water supplies, especially in times of drought, for areas that do not receive the storms' full fury. Similarly, hurricanes that hit the west coast of Mexico, locally known as *chubascos,* and cross the Sierra Madre Oriental into western Texas provide useful inflow to Amistad and Falcon reservoirs, which store water for the lower Rio Grande Valley (Bomar 1995).

With its extreme swings in annual precipitation, Texas is a land of both floods and droughts. Although the epidemic of droughts in the 1930s forced many "dust bowl" farmers and ranchers from their land, the Texas "drought of record," accompanied by scorching summer temperatures, occurred between 1950 and 1956 (NOAA 2004; Stahle and Cleaveland 1988). Elmer Kelton (1973) vividly painted this period in his award-winning novel, *The Time It Never Rained,* about the struggle of a Texas ranching

family to survive on the Edwards Plateau. In 1987, more than thirty years after the 1950s drought and almost thirty years after its founding, the Edwards Underground Water District formulated the state's first regionwide Drought Management Plan to try to mitigate the vagaries of the recurring Central Texas droughts in the face of a fast-growing population. In reaction to the acute drought the year before, in 1997 the Texas legislature adopted Senate Bill 1, "The Water Bill," that mandated water conservation planning for large water users, required public water suppliers to draft drought contingency plans, and limited interbasin transfers. These water restrictions have been enforced during drought periods that occurred in such years as 1998, 2000, 2004, and 2006 (NCDC 2004; TWDB 2002, 2006; TCEQ 2004; Texas State Historical Association 2006; Texas Synergy 2006; *Austin American-Statesman* 2006).

Like floods and droughts, the removal of underground water has caused serious problems. In the early 1940s, studies showed that the land area around Baytown and Texas City along the shores of Galveston Bay had subsided between 1.6 and 3.2 feet since the turn of the century. In the two decades that followed, local governments began making the link between land subsidence and groundwater withdrawal in the fast-growing Houston-Galveston area. The "space race" population boom in the Houston area resulted in so much groundwater pumping that some parts of the metro, particularly near Clear Lake, experienced ground subsidence of more than 15 feet, exacerbating the flood hazard of those areas. In 1973, Galveston began switching from groundwater sources to Lake Houston's surface water; and in 1975, the legislature established the Harris-Galveston Subsidence District to prevent land subsidence by managing the withdrawal of groundwater through a permit system (Harris-Galveston Subsidence District 2006; USGS 2004–2006). In far West Texas, parts of El Paso east of the Franklin Mountains have experienced subsidence associated with decades of groundwater withdrawals from the Hueco-Bolson Aquifer. This desert subsidence is hazardous to structures because it creates cracks in the land, or "earth fissures," up to 1 foot wide and extending for hundreds of feet (Haywood 1995).

Shoreline Erosion
Overview of Study Areas

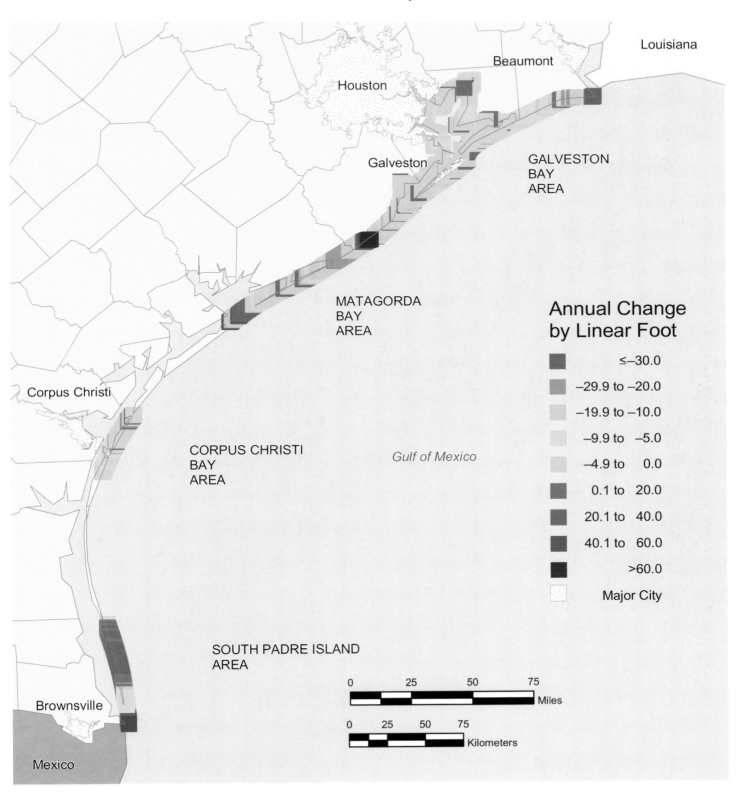

Louisiana

Beaumont

Houston

GALVESTON
BAY
AREA

Galveston

MATAGORDA
BAY
AREA

Corpus Christi

CORPUS CHRISTI
BAY
AREA

Gulf of Mexico

Annual Change by Linear Foot

■	≤–30.0
■	–29.9 to –20.0
■	–19.9 to –10.0
■	–9.9 to –5.0
■	–4.9 to 0.0
■	0.1 to 20.0
■	20.1 to 40.0
■	40.1 to 60.0
■	>60.0
▦	Major City

SOUTH PADRE ISLAND
AREA

Brownsville

Mexico

0   25   50   75
Miles

0   25   50   75
Kilometers

Source: U.S. Geological Survey, 2001.

Shoreline Erosion
Focus on Study Areas

GALVESTON BAY

MATAGORDA BAY

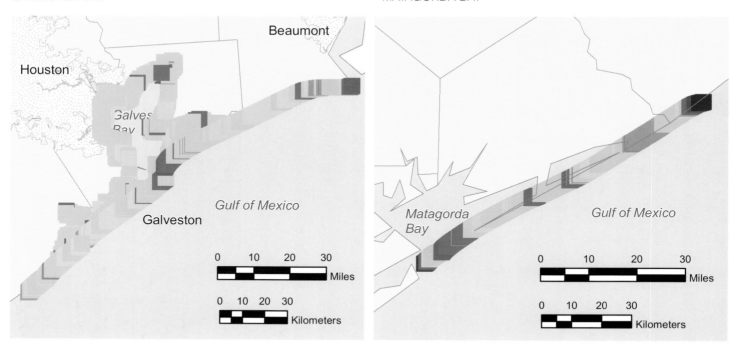

Beaumont

Houston

Galves
Bay

Gulf of Mexico

Galveston

0 10 20 30 Miles

0 10 20 30 Kilometers

Matagorda
Bay

Gulf of Mexico

0 10 20 30 Miles

0 10 20 30 Kilometers

Annual Change by Linear Foot

≤ -30.0	-9.9– -5.0	20.1–40.0	Major City
-29.9– -20.0	-4.9– 0.0	40.1–60.0	
-19.9– -10.0	0.1–20.0	>60.0	

CORPUS CHRISTI BAY

SOUTH PADRE ISLAND

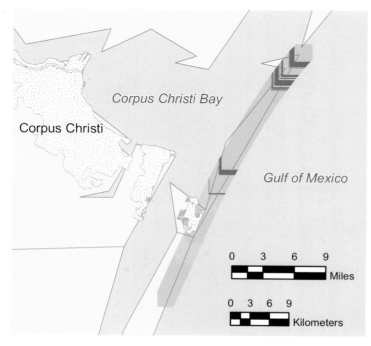

Corpus Christi Bay

Corpus Christi

Gulf of Mexico

0 3 6 9 Miles

0 3 6 9 Kilometers

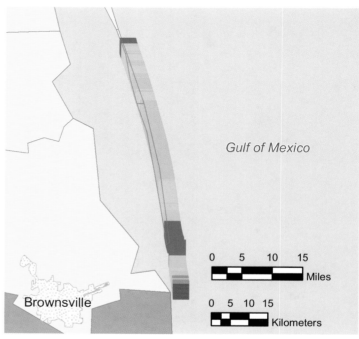

Gulf of Mexico

Brownsville

0 5 10 15 Miles

0 5 10 15 Kilometers

Source: U.S. Geological Survey, 2001.

Floodplain Zones

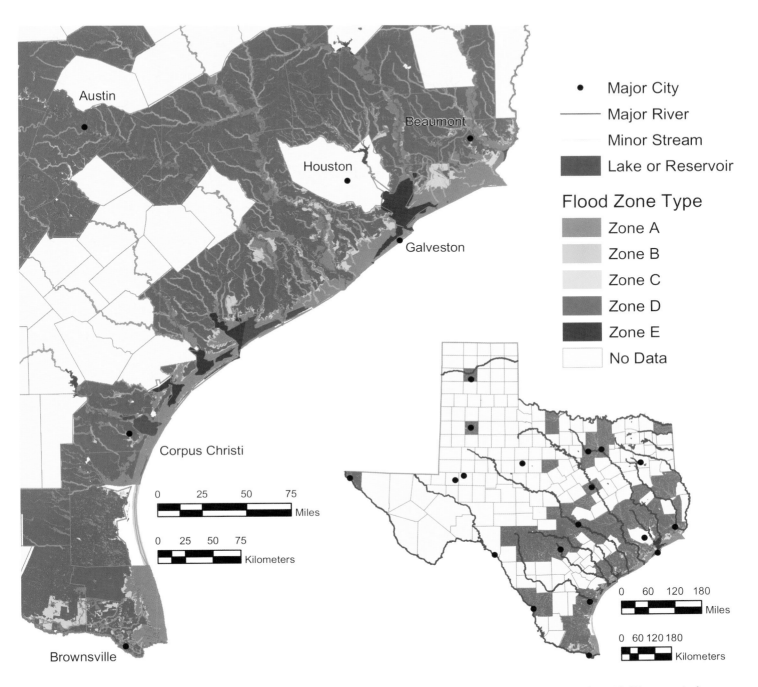

Note: Zone A: 100-year flooding (1 percent probability of being inundated in any year) without wave action; 19.07 percent of flood zones.

Zone B: 100-year flooding with wave action; 0.57 percent of flood zones.

Zone C: 500-year flooding (0.2 percent probability of being inundated in any year) or 100-year flooding but less affected than Zone A in terms of area (<1 square mile) and depth (<1 foot) and because protective levees from 100-year flooding are in place; 2.2 percent of flood zones.

Zone D: Outside the 100- and 500-year floodplains; 76.46 percent of flood zones.

Zone E: A body of water, such as a pond, lake, ocean, etc., with no defined flood hazard; 1.7 percent of flood zones.

Source: Federal Insurance and Mitigation Administration, 2000.

Selected Floodplains
Downtown Areas

DALLAS

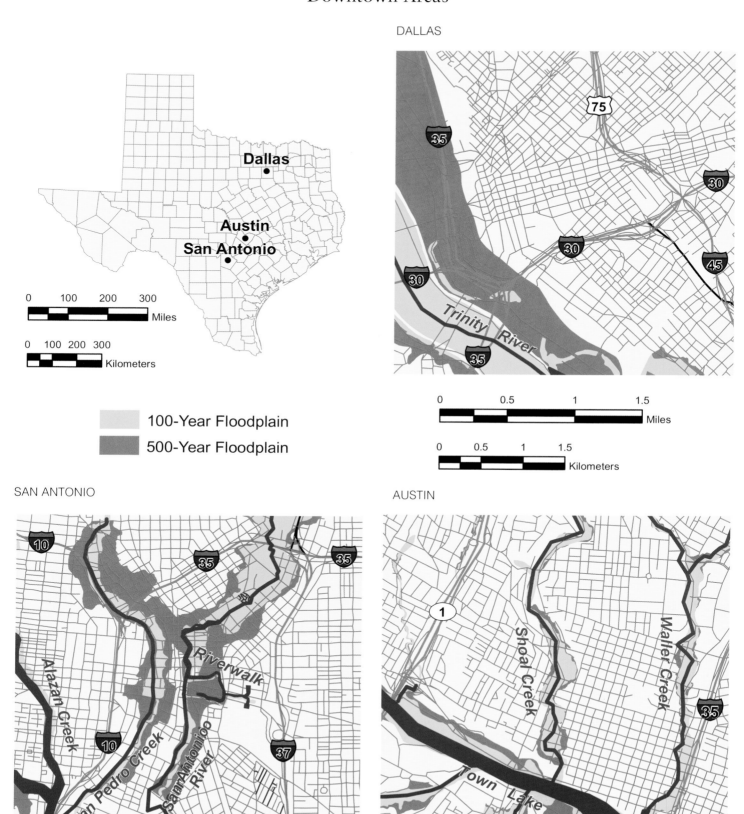

100-Year Floodplain
500-Year Floodplain

SAN ANTONIO

AUSTIN

Sources: Federal Insurance and Mitigation Administration, 2000; U.S. Census Bureau, 2000.

Historic Floods, 1853–2002

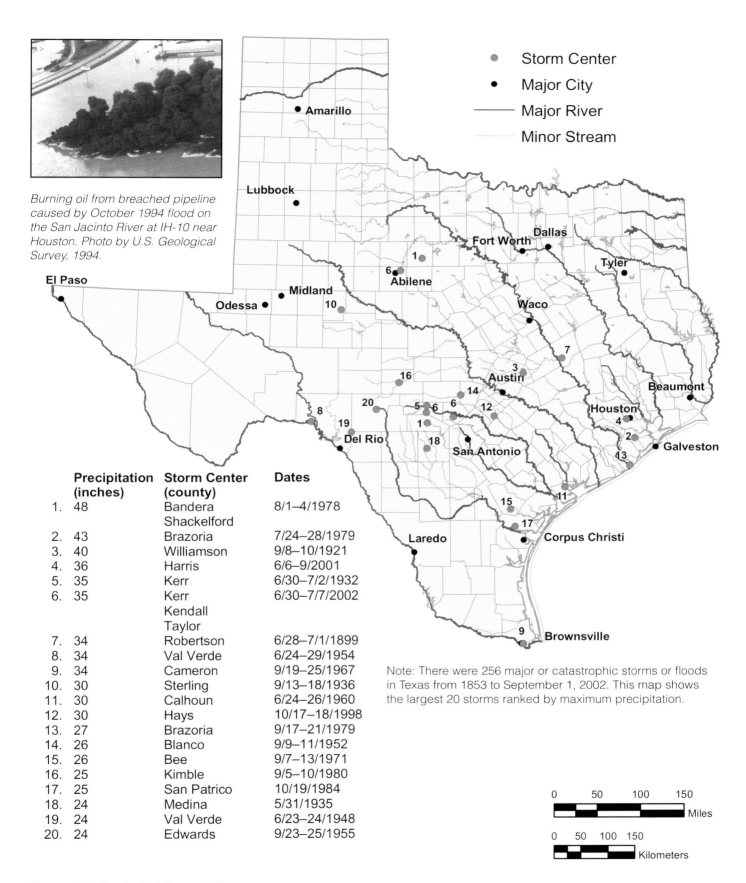

Burning oil from breached pipeline caused by October 1994 flood on the San Jacinto River at IH-10 near Houston. Photo by U.S. Geological Survey, 1994.

Legend
- Storm Center
- Major City
- Major River
- Minor Stream

	Precipitation (inches)	Storm Center (county)	Dates
1.	48	Bandera Shackelford	8/1–4/1978
2.	43	Brazoria	7/24–28/1979
3.	40	Williamson	9/8–10/1921
4.	36	Harris	6/6–9/2001
5.	35	Kerr	6/30–7/2/1932
6.	35	Kerr Kendall Taylor	6/30–7/7/2002
7.	34	Robertson	6/28–7/1/1899
8.	34	Val Verde	6/24–29/1954
9.	34	Cameron	9/19–25/1967
10.	30	Sterling	9/13–18/1936
11.	30	Calhoun	6/24–26/1960
12.	30	Hays	10/17–18/1998
13.	27	Brazoria	9/17–21/1979
14.	26	Blanco	9/9–11/1952
15.	26	Bee	9/7–13/1971
16.	25	Kimble	9/5–10/1980
17.	25	San Patrico	10/19/1984
18.	24	Medina	5/31/1935
19.	24	Val Verde	6/23–24/1948
20.	24	Edwards	9/23–25/1955

Note: There were 256 major or catastrophic storms or floods in Texas from 1853 to September 1, 2002. This map shows the largest 20 storms ranked by maximum precipitation.

Source: U.S. Geological Survey, 2002.

Floods from Storms, 1853–2002

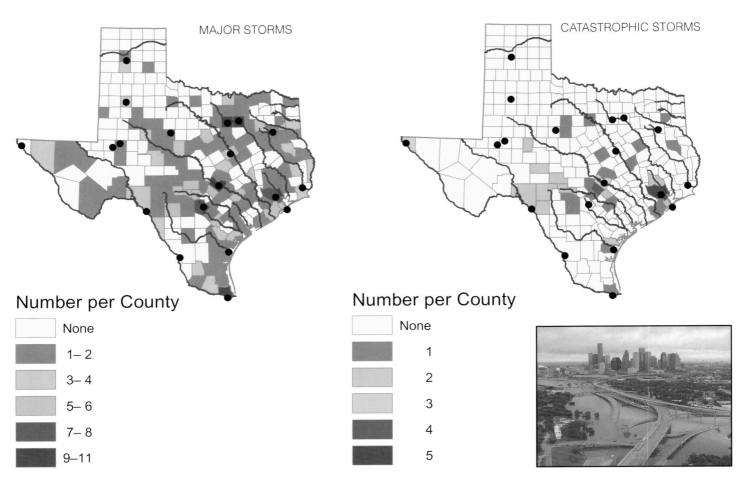

MAJOR STORMS

CATASTROPHIC STORMS

Number per County

- None
- 1– 2
- 3– 4
- 5– 6
- 7– 8
- 9–11

Number per County

- None
- 1
- 2
- 3
- 4
- 5

Flooding from Tropical Storm Allison in Houston, June 6–9, 2001. Photo by Houston Chronicle, 2001.

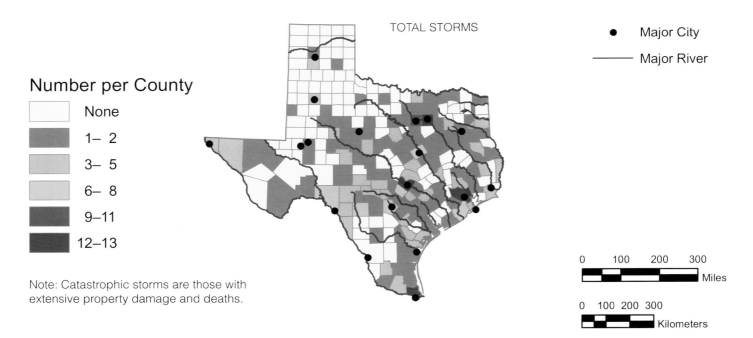

TOTAL STORMS

Number per County

- None
- 1– 2
- 3– 5
- 6– 8
- 9–11
- 12–13

Note: Catastrophic storms are those with extensive property damage and deaths.

- ● Major City
- —— Major River

| 0 | 100 | 200 | 300 |
Miles

| 0 | 100 | 200 | 300 |
Kilometers

Source: U.S. Geological Survey, 2002.

Flash Floods, 1986–99

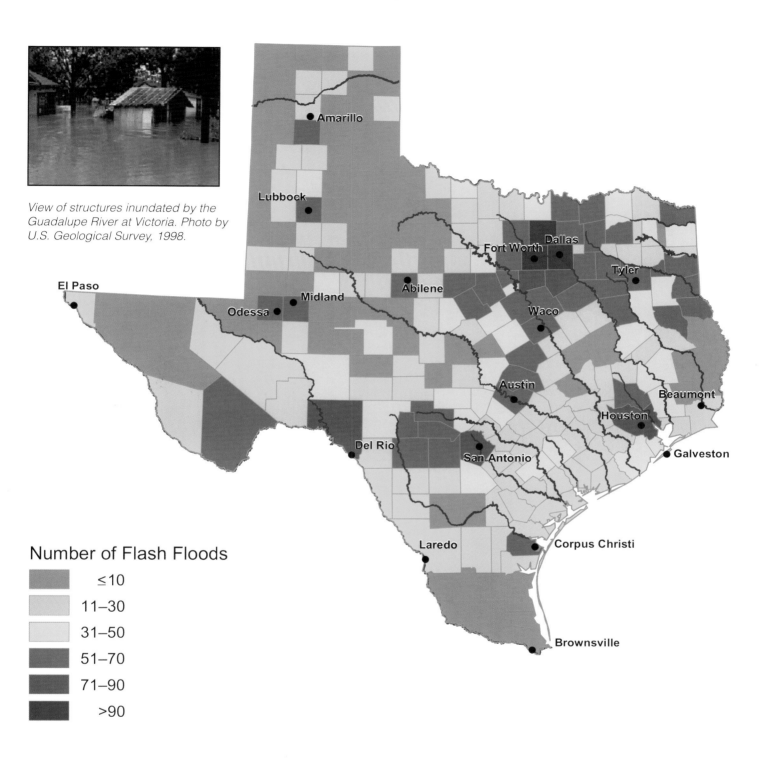

View of structures inundated by the Guadalupe River at Victoria. Photo by U.S. Geological Survey, 1998.

Number of Flash Floods

	≤10
	11–30
	31–50
	51–70
	71–90
	>90

Note: A flash flood is a sudden local flood of great volume and short duration caused by heavy rains during a short period.

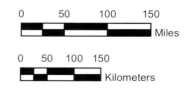

Source: National Weather Service, 2000.

Hurricane Paths
Most Damaging Storms, 1950–2000

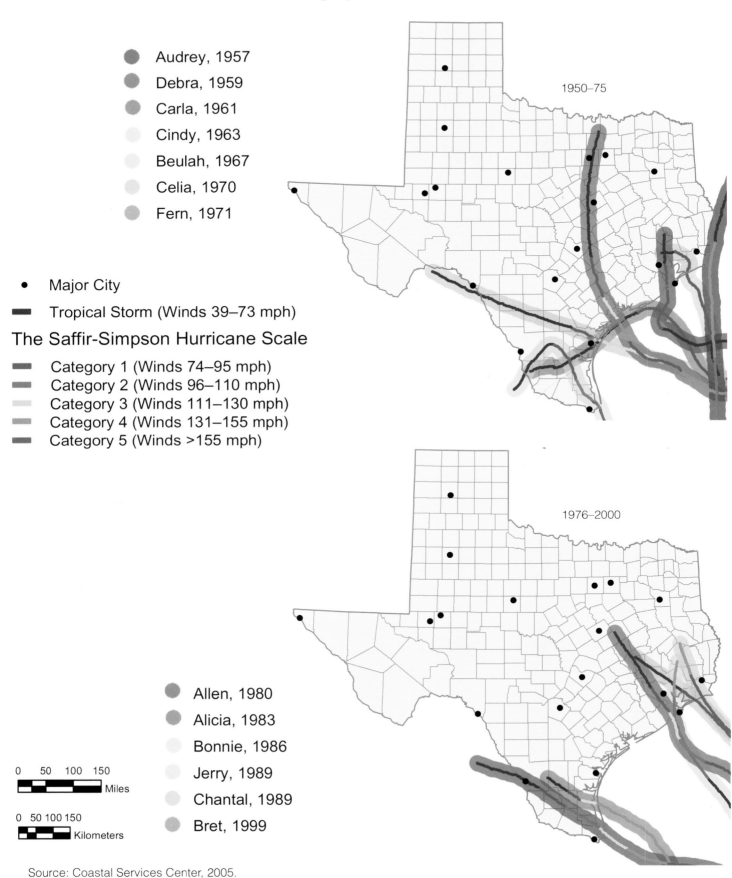

Audrey, 1957
Debra, 1959
Carla, 1961
Cindy, 1963
Beulah, 1967
Celia, 1970
Fern, 1971

• Major City

▬ Tropical Storm (Winds 39–73 mph)

The Saffir-Simpson Hurricane Scale

▬ Category 1 (Winds 74–95 mph)
▬ Category 2 (Winds 96–110 mph)
▬ Category 3 (Winds 111–130 mph)
▬ Category 4 (Winds 131–155 mph)
▬ Category 5 (Winds >155 mph)

1950–75

1976–2000

Allen, 1980
Alicia, 1983
Bonnie, 1986
Jerry, 1989
Chantal, 1989
Bret, 1999

0   50 100 150
Miles

0 50 100 150
Kilometers

Source: Coastal Services Center, 2005.

Hurricane Intensity
Most Severely Affected Counties

Hurricane winds are usually strongest on the right side of the storm in the northern hemisphere, as shown by the distribution of counties affected by Hurricane Carla. Winds from Hurricane Carla were the leading cause of damage. Although rainfall averaged only 10 to 16 inches, winds were recorded at up to 170 miles per hour. In Texas, Carla caused $300 million in damage as well as the deaths of 43 people.

In 1967, Hurricane Beulah quickly decreased from a Category 5 to a Category 2 storm once it made landfall, which lessened the amount of wind damage. Severe flooding and many tornadoes (approximately 95) caused most of the damage. Rainfall in some areas reached up to 30 inches. Storm damage from Beulah was about $20 million, but damage from flooding reached $100 million.

- Major City
- Tropical Storm (Winds 39–73 mph)

The Saffir-Simpson Hurricane Scale
- Category 1 (Winds 74–95 mph)
- Category 2 (Winds 96–110 mph)
- Category 3 (Winds 111–130 mph)
- Category 4 (Winds 131–155 mph)
- Category 5 (Winds >155 mph)

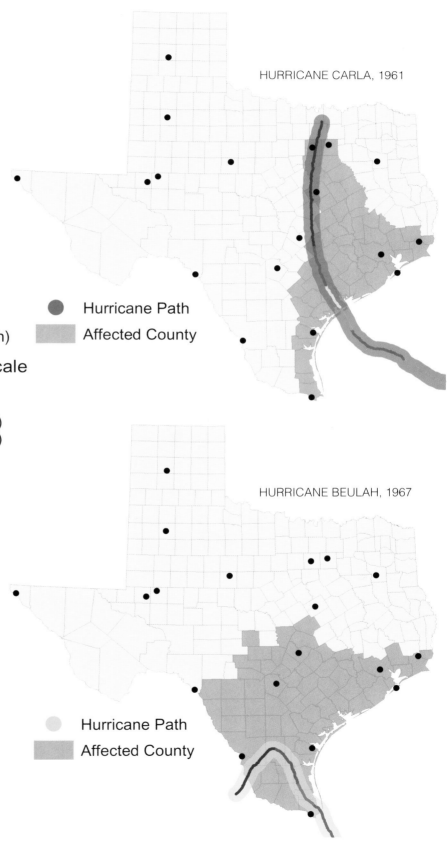

HURRICANE CARLA, 1961

Hurricane Path
Affected County

HURRICANE BEULAH, 1967

Hurricane Path
Affected County

Source: Coastal Services Center, 2005.

Major Droughts
National Weather Service Climatic Divisions

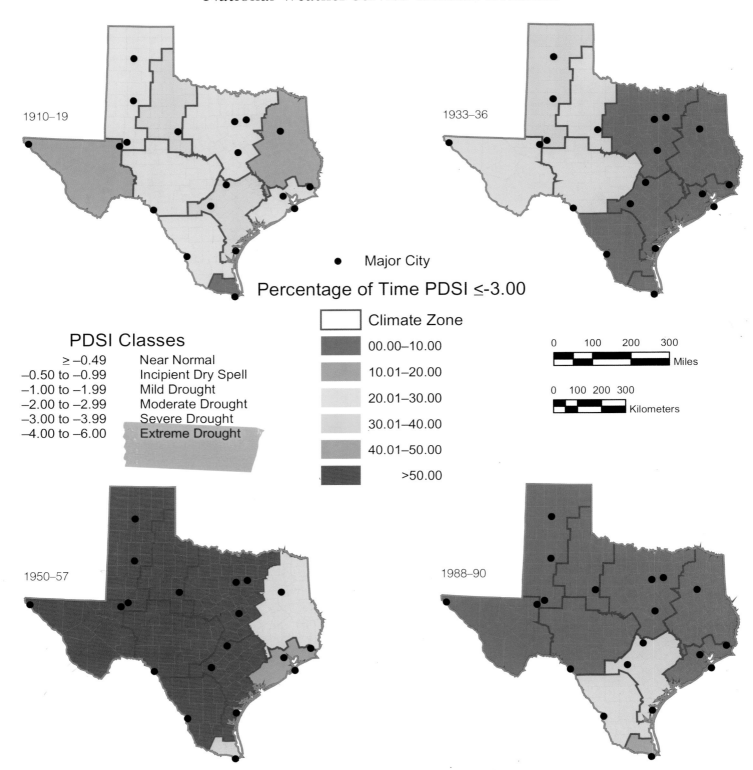

1910–19

1933–36

● Major City

Percentage of Time PDSI ≤-3.00

PDSI Classes

≥ −0.49	Near Normal
−0.50 to −0.99	Incipient Dry Spell
−1.00 to −1.99	Mild Drought
−2.00 to −2.99	Moderate Drought
−3.00 to −3.99	Severe Drought
−4.00 to −6.00	Extreme Drought

Climate Zone
00.00–10.00
10.01–20.00
20.01–30.00
30.01–40.00
40.01–50.00
>50.00

0   100   200   300
Miles

0   100 200 300
Kilometers

1950–57

1988–90

These maps are based on the Palmer Drought Severity Index (PDSI), which is calculated monthly by the National Weather Service climatic division using an algorithm that accounts for precipitation and temperature recordings and the local available moisture in the soil. The drought periods illustrated highlight the percentage of time during a given drought period when the PDSI value ranged from −3.00 to −6.00 (Severe to Extreme Drought).

Source: National Climate Data Center, 2004.

Public Water Supply Systems
Affected by Drought, 2004

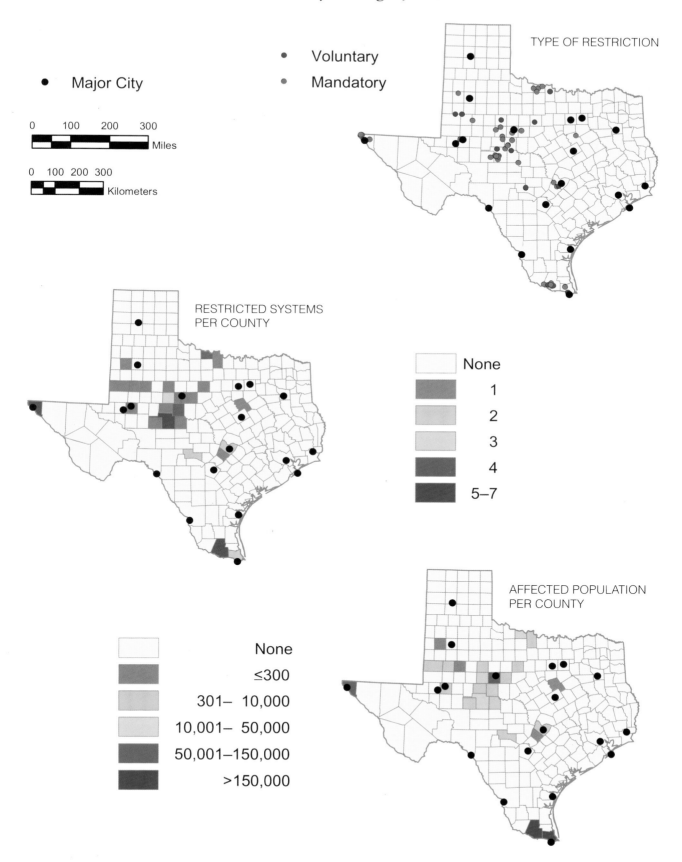

TYPE OF RESTRICTION

- Major City
- Voluntary
- Mandatory

0   100   200   300
Miles

0   100 200 300
Kilometers

RESTRICTED SYSTEMS
PER COUNTY

None
1
2
3
4
5–7

AFFECTED POPULATION
PER COUNTY

None
≤300
301– 10,000
10,001– 50,000
50,001–150,000
>150,000

Source: Texas Commission on Environmental Quality, 2004.

Per Capita Water Use in Drought, 2000

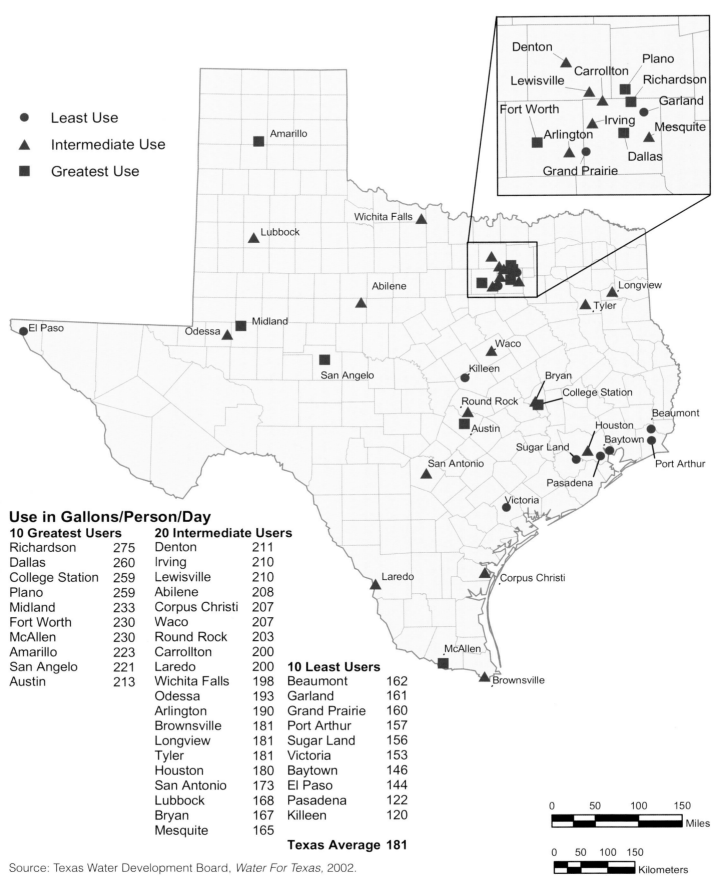

● Least Use

▲ Intermediate Use

■ Greatest Use

Amarillo

Lubbock

Wichita Falls

Abilene

El Paso

Odessa   Midland

San Angelo

Waco

Killeen

Round Rock

Austin

San Antonio

Victoria

Laredo

McAllen

Brownsville

Corpus Christi

Longview

Tyler

Bryan

College Station

Sugar Land   Houston

Pasadena   Baytown

Beaumont

Port Arthur

Inset:
Denton

Lewisville   Carrollton   Plano   Richardson

Fort Worth   Irving   Garland

Arlington   Mesquite

Grand Prairie   Dallas

Use in Gallons/Person/Day

10 Greatest Users
Richardson	275
Dallas	260
College Station	259
Plano	259
Midland	233
Fort Worth	230
McAllen	230
Amarillo	223
San Angelo	221
Austin	213

20 Intermediate Users
Denton	211
Irving	210
Lewisville	210
Abilene	208
Corpus Christi	207
Waco	207
Round Rock	203
Carrollton	200
Laredo	200
Wichita Falls	198
Odessa	193
Arlington	190
Brownsville	181
Longview	181
Tyler	181
Houston	180
San Antonio	173
Lubbock	168
Bryan	167
Mesquite	165

10 Least Users
Beaumont	162
Garland	161
Grand Prairie	160
Port Arthur	157
Sugar Land	156
Victoria	153
Baytown	146
El Paso	144
Pasadena	122
Killeen	120

Texas Average 181

0   50   100   150
Miles

0   50   100   150
Kilometers

Source: Texas Water Development Board, *Water For Texas*, 2002.

Groundwater Overdraft Subsidence
Houston-Galveston Area, 1906–2000

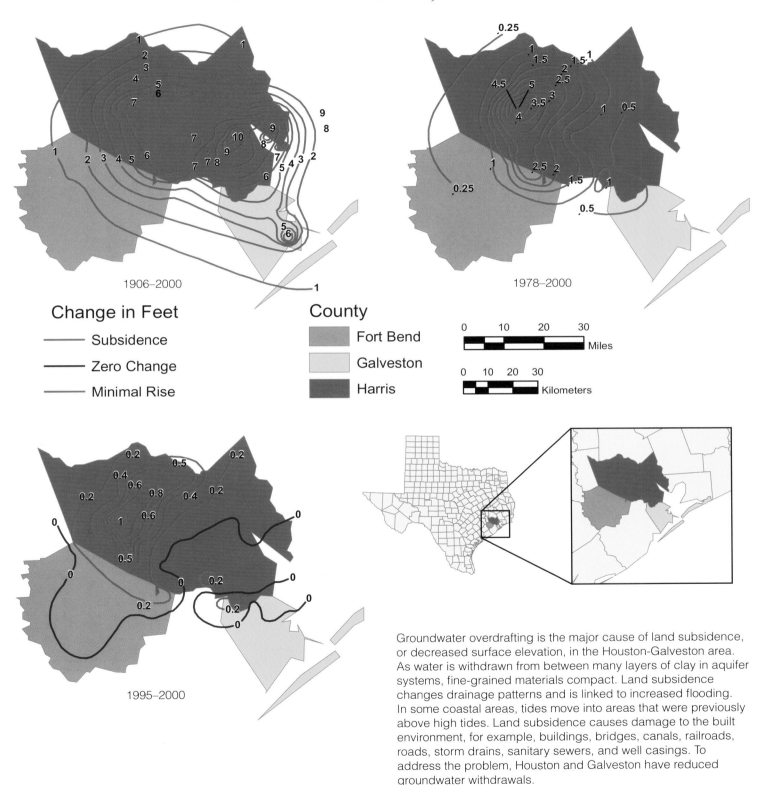

1906–2000

1978–2000

Change in Feet

— Subsidence

— Zero Change

— Minimal Rise

County

- Fort Bend
- Galveston
- Harris

0	10	20	30	
				Miles

0	10	20	30	
				Kilometers

1995–2000

Groundwater overdrafting is the major cause of land subsidence, or decreased surface elevation, in the Houston-Galveston area. As water is withdrawn from between many layers of clay in aquifer systems, fine-grained materials compact. Land subsidence changes drainage patterns and is linked to increased flooding. In some coastal areas, tides move into areas that were previously above high tides. Land subsidence causes damage to the built environment, for example, buildings, bridges, canals, railroads, roads, storm drains, sanitary sewers, and well casings. To address the problem, Houston and Galveston have reduced groundwater withdrawals.

Sources: Leake, 2004; U.S. Geological Survey, 2005; Harris-Galveston Coastal Subsidence District, 2005.

4 Water Quantity and Quality

BEYOND THE QUART OR SO OF WATER that humans biologically need every day, even the simplest lifestyle requires far greater amounts of water for human hygiene, cooking, and washing. Since earliest times, irrigation has increased crop production in all but the wettest regions. Similarly, other economic activities, such as manufacturing, mining, and ranching, require large amounts of water. During the past half century, water has also become an increasingly important medium for recreational and aesthetic-based activities. As the population of Texas has increased, so has its water consumption, creating an ever-enlarging challenge for the state to provide its citizens with adequate sources of clean water. Conservation, reuse, and innovative new sources of water, such as desalinated water, will continue to be critical themes in the future of Texas water quantity and quality (TWDB 2007; TPWD 2007; U.S. Census 2005).

Texas settlement has always been dependent on reliable water supplies. Archeological evidence indicates that humans have occupied San Marcos Springs for more than ten thousand years (Shiner 1983). In the centuries before European contact, Native Americans developed pueblo settlements based on irrigation along the Rio Grande and Pecos River. Spanish settlement, in all but the easternmost part of the state, also depended on perennial streams for basic water needs and agricultural irrigation. Restored remnants of Spanish irrigation systems, or acequias, are featured at the San Antonio Missions National Historical Park. The life-giving acequias not only irrigated crops but also powered waterwheels that ground grain and drove primitive machinery such as lathes and blacksmith bellows (de la Teja 1995; Oliver 2004).

Initial Anglo migration into Texas, beginning with the Austin colony in 1821, followed the Spanish model of locating settlements at reliable water sources. Settlers established communities along perennial streams. In fact, it is difficult today to identify a Texas city founded before 1870 that was not located along a perennial stream. A notable example of this dependence is demonstrated by the location of cities along the Balcones Escarpment spring line (Petersen 1995). After the Spanish established San Antonio, settlements "sprung up" along the spring line at New Braunfels at Comal Springs in 1844, San Marcos Springs in 1847, and Georgetown in 1848 (Tyler 1996; Brune 2002; Heitmuller and Reece 2003).

Advances in technology, beginning with the wind-powered pump—the windmill—facilitated settlement at waterless locations with shallow groundwater. These low-flow pumps provided sufficient water for livestock, steam locomotives, and small settlements beginning in the late 1800s. Representative of this era of water resources development are the founding of many towns on the Llano Estacado (Staked Plains) of Panhandle Texas, such as Lubbock in 1884 and Amarillo in 1887. Early in the twentieth century, the development of the engine-driven centrifugal pump produced a revolution in Texas water use, agriculture, and settlement. Whereas a windmill could yield a few gallons of water per hour, the new pumps could produce hundreds of gallons per minute. This exponential increase in pump efficiency meant that large fertile areas of West Texas and Panhandle Texas could be opened up to intensive crop agriculture and that crops in many of the wetter portions of Texas could receive supplemental irrigation to increase yields and provide drought protection (Beaumont 1985). Between 1930 and 1950, for instance, irrigated acreage and groundwater use increased dramatically, and the number of water wells drilled annually soared to almost thirty-five hundred in the midst of the great drought of the 1950s (TWDB 2004).

Since the early 1900s most rivers in Texas have been dammed to capture floodwaters to reduce downstream flooding and to provide water supply during dry periods. Private funds initially supported the building of dams, such as Medina Dam in 1911–12, but increased costs and concern for safety resulted in government assuming the role of financing, building, and operating all but the smallest dams. The U.S. Army Corps of Engineers, the Texas river authorities, and the U.S. Bureau of Reclamation have been the state's major dam builders. The U.S. Soil Conservation Service, presently called the U.S. Natural Resource Conservation Service, built numerous flood-control detention dams in drainage areas of less than 100 square miles. Most of these smaller flood-control dams do not usually store water. The era of dam building peaked in the 1950s and 1960s, and federally subsidized dam building declined precipitously after the late 1970s when local entities were required to pay higher percentages of dam construction costs (Thompson 1999).

The U.S. Geological Survey (USGS) established in the late 1800s a network of stream gaging stations across the country to monitor both the quantity and quality of surface water and groundwater (USGS National Water Inventory System 2005). Approximately 440 USGS stations currently measure stream flow and lake levels in Texas. Most of these sites report their status every fifteen to sixty minutes via a public USGS Web site (http://waterdata.usgs.gov/tx/nwis/rt). Moreover, about 150 USGS sites measure water-quality parameters. These data are exceptionally useful in estimating current water supplies and projecting near- to midterm water inventories; the information is also critical to monitoring immediate flood threats, creating flood and flow histories, and identifying historic changes in stream characteristics. Because of budgetary constraints, however, the USGS has discontinued more than 800 other discharge sites and over 230 water quality stations (USGS 2006). The Texas Commission on Environmental Quality (TCEQ) has a complementary set of sites that monitor water quality by employing both full-time staff and volunteers through its Texas Watch Program (TCEQ 2005).

The rapid settlement and extensive economic development of Texas have strained surface water supplies. Fights over livestock watering holes broke out during drought times in the post–Civil War cattle boom and were the focus of innumerable Hollywood films, such as *The Big Country* (1958). Diversion of surface streams for irrigation exacerbated the water crises to the point that legislative remedy was sought in the 1880s. These surface water battles triggered the development of the principle of "prior appropriation." In 1887 the state initiated the "first in time, first in right" water allocation system on a stream-by-stream basis. The system was expanded statewide by the 1913 Texas Water Code, still the basic docu-

ment for managing water in Texas today. The desire to manage water resources development on a basinwide level led in the 1930s to the establishment of river authorities. These quasi-public organizations have played a fundamental role in the planning, building, and operating of water systems and electric supplies in the state ever since (Kaiser 1996a, 1996b).

Just as uncontrolled use of surface water necessitated its regulation, the exploitation of groundwater has led incrementally to more public oversight. Although the "rule of capture," giving landowners the legal right to use the water under their land, is still in effect, the original interpretation of what has come to be known as the "law of the biggest pump" has gradually shifted to more restrictive rights in a series of steps beginning with the 1949 Underground Conservation District Act. Initially, the Groundwater Conservation Districts had authority to gather data only, but the legislature extended their power in 1985, 1999, and 2001. The 1985 act gave districts the authority to tax nondomestic and livestock uses of water (Kaiser 1986). The 1999 legislation allowed for countywide districts, and the 2001 Senate Bill 2 required new water users to demonstrate that they would not impinge on the historic users of an aquifer's water (Texas Bar CLE 2005). In the early 1990s, lawsuits based on the federal Endangered Species Act forced Texas to create the Edwards Aquifer Authority in 1993, which has a prior appropriation permit system for all nondomestic and livestock water uses. The Edwards Aquifer Authority incorporates mandatory, phased-in pumping reductions when water in the aquifer drops below certain specified levels (Earl and Votteler 2005).

Today, the available quantity of water and its quality in Texas are foci of concern for the federal government, particularly through the efforts of the USGS, as well as state agencies led by the Texas Water Development Board (TWDB) and the TCEQ. The TWDB leads in the planning, funding assistance, and educational efforts regarding thoughtful development of the state's water resources throughout its sixteen water management regions authorized by Senate Bill 1 in 1997. The TCEQ ensures that Texans have clean water. Both agencies monitor the quantity and quality of the state's water resources and publish a wide variety of information, such as water supply indices and availability; water allocation, diversion rights, and usage; and water wells drilled and groundwater quality (TWDB 2005; TCEQ 2005).

Spanish-Mexican Acequias

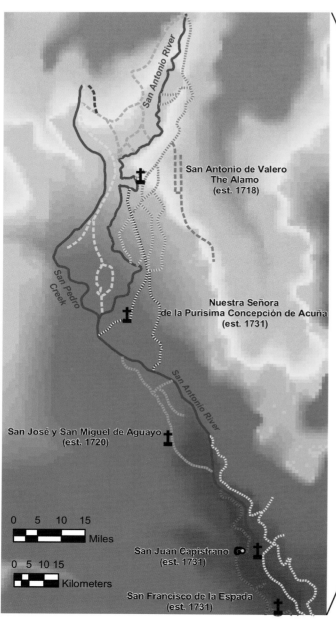

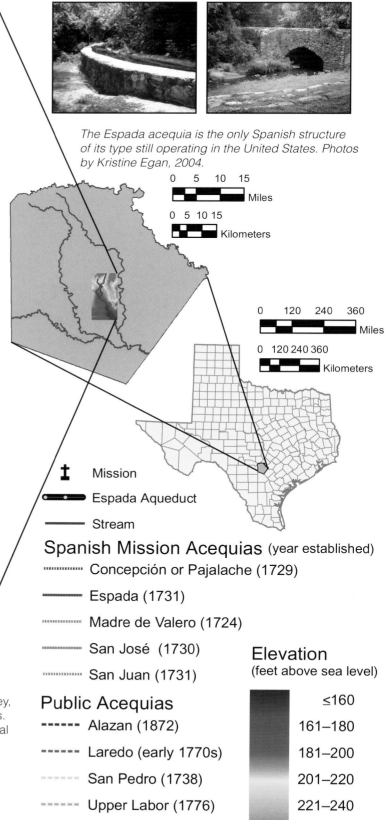

The Espada acequia is the only Spanish structure of its type still operating in the United States. Photos by Kristine Egan, 2004.

Mission

Espada Aqueduct

Stream

Spanish Mission Acequias (year established)

Concepción or Pajalache (1729)

Espada (1731)

Madre de Valero (1724)

San José (1730)

San Juan (1731)

Public Acequias

Alazan (1872)

Laredo (early 1770s)

San Pedro (1738)

Upper Labor (1776)

Valley (1872)

Elevation
(feet above sea level)

	≤160
	161–180
	181–200
	201–220
	221–240
	>240

The early Spanish Franciscan missionaries brought to Texas sophisticated knowledge required to construct acequias, or irrigation ditches. The acequias were an essential element to agricultural efforts in areas of sparse rainfall. Because of the establishment of several missions in the San Antonio River Valley, the region had the most extensive network of acequias in Texas. In addition to those built by the missions, there were also several public and ancillary acequias in the area.

Sources: Oliver, 2004; Guerra, 1987; Minor, 1968; de la Teja, 1995.

USGS Real-Time Gaging Stations, 2005

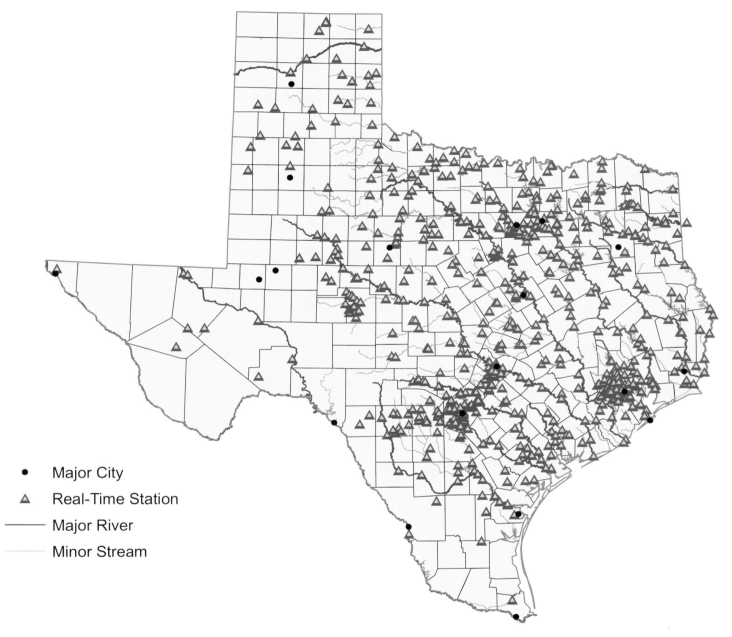

- ●   Major City
- △   Real-Time Station
- ——   Major River
- ——   Minor Stream

USGS maintains various categories of real-time stations, including groundwater, stream flow, precipitation, water quality, and lake or reservoir. Real-time stations typically record data at 15-minute to one-hour intervals and relay the data to USGS offices every one to four hours via satellite, telephone, and/or radio.

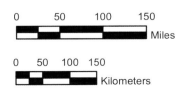

Source: U.S. Geological Survey, National Water Inventory System, 2005.

Surface Water Supply Index, 2002

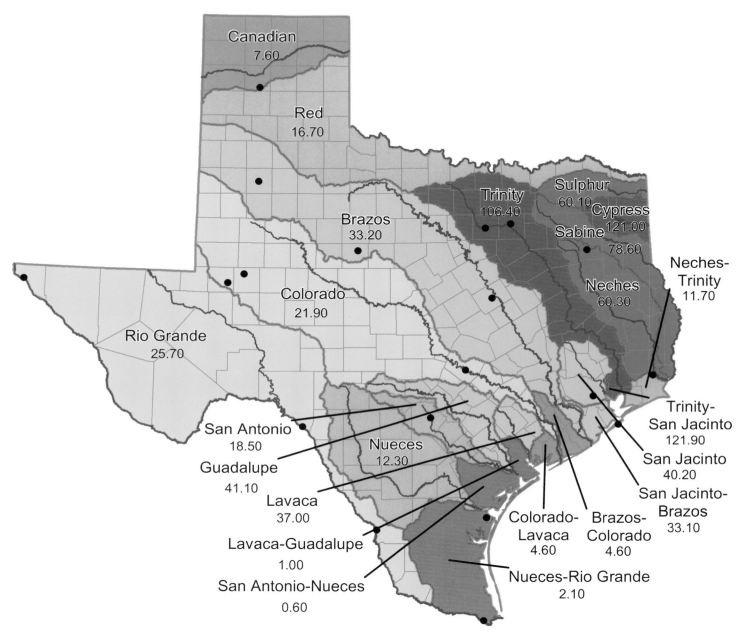

Canadian
7.60

Red
16.70

Trinity
106.40

Sulphur
60.10

Cypress
121.00

Sabine
78.60

Brazos
33.20

Neches-
Trinity
11.70

Colorado
21.90

Neches
60.30

Rio Grande
25.70

Trinity-
San Jacinto
121.90

San Jacinto
40.20

San Antonio
18.50

Nueces
12.30

San Jacinto-
Brazos
33.10

Guadalupe
41.10

Lavaca
37.00

Colorado-
Lavaca
4.60

Brazos-
Colorado
4.60

Lavaca-Guadalupe
1.00

San Antonio-Nueces
0.60

Nueces-Rio Grande
2.10

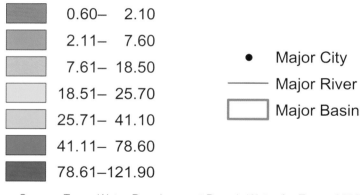

Acre-Feet/Year/Square Mile

	0.60– 2.10
	2.11– 7.60
	7.61– 18.50
	18.51– 25.70
	25.71– 41.10
	41.11– 78.60
	78.61–121.90

● Major City

— Major River

☐ Major Basin

Note: The surface water supply index quantifies river basin water supply density. Coastal river basins tend to have a relatively low surface water supply index because of the deficiency of water supply facilities (e.g., reservoirs).

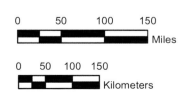

0   50   100   150
▬▬▬▬▬▬▬ Miles

0   50   100 150
▬▬▬▬▬▬▬ Kilometers

Source: Texas Water Development Board, *Water for Texas,* 2002.

Surface Water Availability, 2002

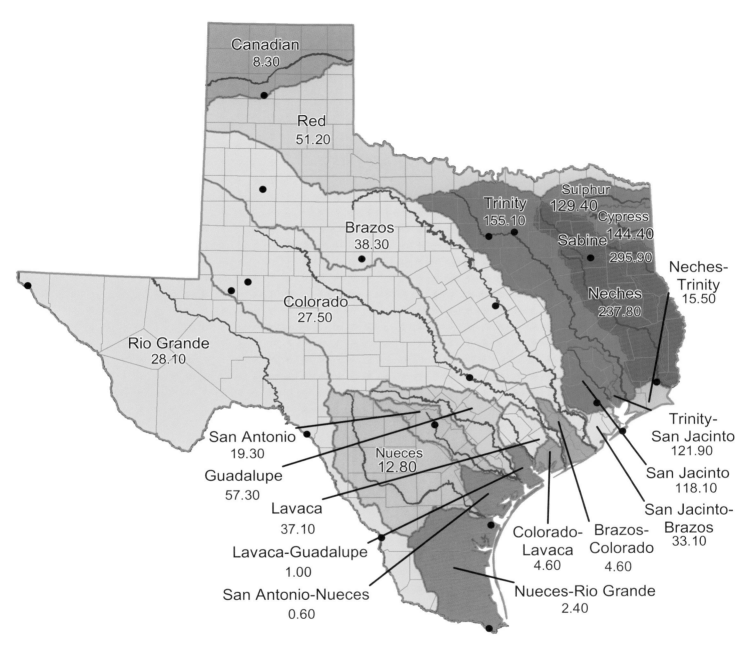

Canadian
8.30

Red
51.20

Brazos
38.30

Trinity
155.10

Sulphur
129.40

Cypress
144.40

Sabine
295.90

Neches-
Trinity
15.50

Neches
237.80

Colorado
27.50

Rio Grande
28.10

San Antonio
19.30

Guadalupe
57.30

Lavaca
37.10

Lavaca-Guadalupe
1.00

San Antonio-Nueces
0.60

Nueces
12.80

Colorado-
Lavaca
4.60

Brazos-
Colorado
4.60

Nueces-Rio Grande
2.40

Trinity-
San Jacinto
121.90

San Jacinto
118.10

San Jacinto-
Brazos
33.10

Acre-Feet/Year/Square Mile

	0.60– 2.40
	2.41– 8.30
	8.31– 19.30
	19.31– 38.30
	38.31– 57.30
	57.31–155.10
	155.11–295.90

● Major City

— Major River

▭ Major Basin

Note: The current water supply is determined by factors such as water availability, water rights or contracts, and supply conveyance facility conditions. In 2002, Texas had approximately 14.9 million acre-feet of surface water available.

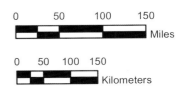

0   50   100   150
Miles

0   50   100   150
Kilometers

Source: Texas Water Development Board, *Water for Texas*, 2002.

Surface Water Allocation, 2004

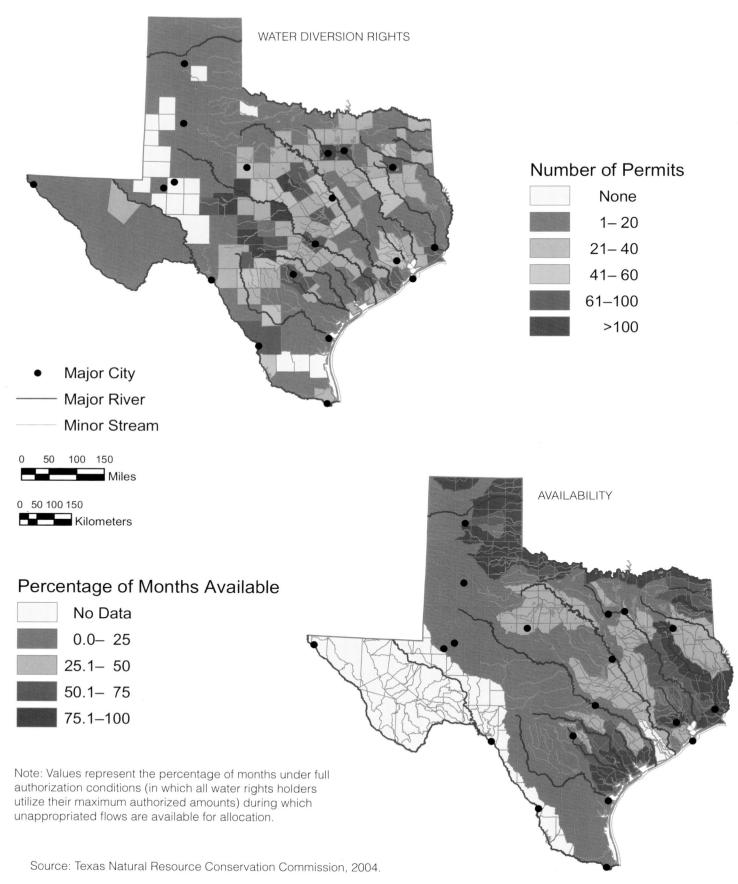

WATER DIVERSION RIGHTS

Number of Permits

	None
	1– 20
	21– 40
	41– 60
	61–100
	>100

● Major City

— Major River

— Minor Stream

0   50   100   150
■■■■ Miles

0   50 100 150
■■■■ Kilometers

AVAILABILITY

Percentage of Months Available

	No Data
	0.0– 25
	25.1– 50
	50.1– 75
	75.1–100

Note: Values represent the percentage of months under full authorization conditions (in which all water rights holders utilize their maximum authorized amounts) during which unappropriated flows are available for allocation.

Source: Texas Natural Resource Conservation Commission, 2004.

Surface Water Quality, 2000

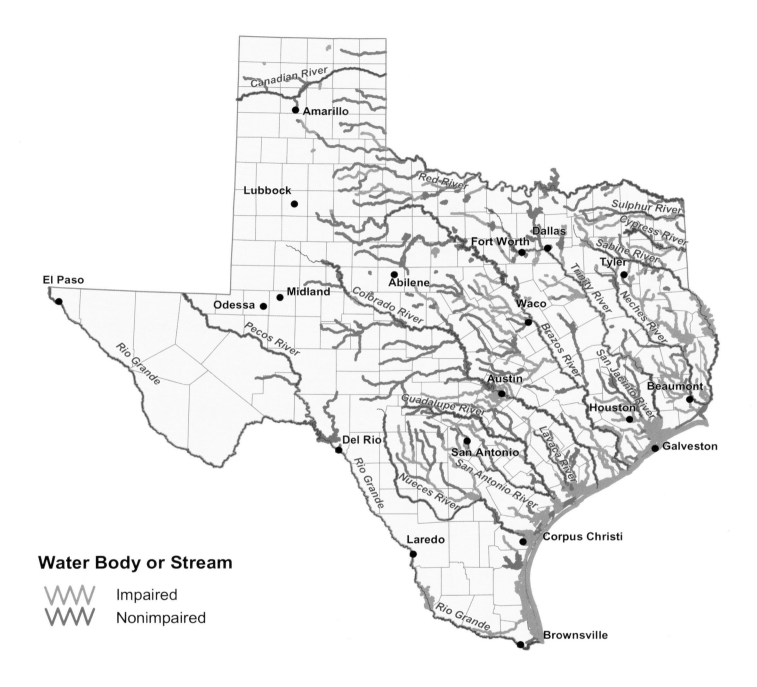

Water Body or Stream

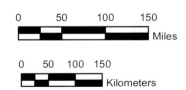

Impaired

Nonimpaired

Note: An impaired segment is a water body that does not meet the Surface Water Quality Standards as listed in Title 30, Chapter 307 of the Texas Administrative Code. The map is not a complete hydrographic representation of Texas; therefore, some stream segments and water bodies appear to be detached.

Source: Texas Commission on Environmental Quality, 2000.

Water Desalination Plants, 2004

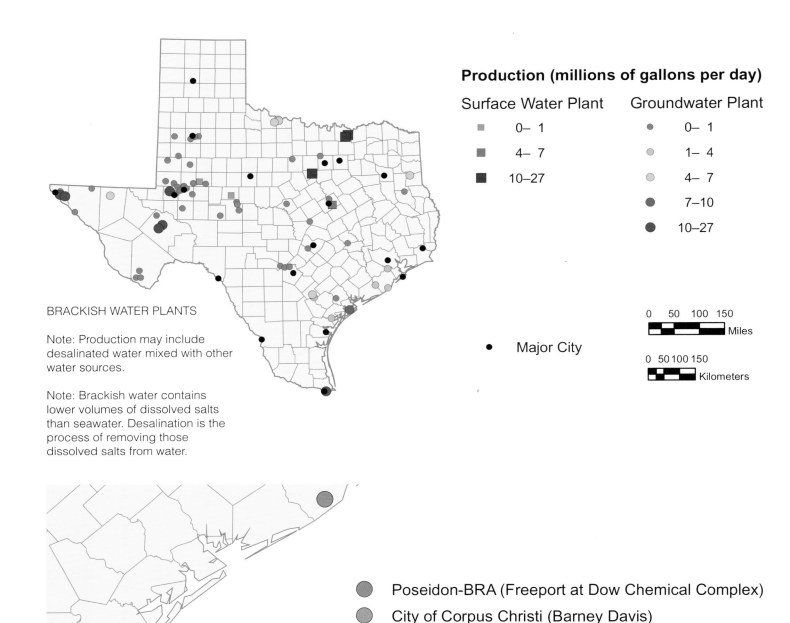

Production (millions of gallons per day)

Surface Water Plant
- 0– 1
- 4– 7
- 10–27

Groundwater Plant
- 0– 1
- 1– 4
- 4– 7
- 7–10
- 10–27

BRACKISH WATER PLANTS

Note: Production may include desalinated water mixed with other water sources.

Note: Brackish water contains lower volumes of dissolved salts than seawater. Desalination is the process of removing those dissolved salts from water.

• Major City

0 50 100 150 Miles

0 50 100 150 Kilometers

Poseidon-BRA (Freeport at Dow Chemical Complex)
City of Corpus Christi (Barney Davis)
Port of Brownsville (Brownsville Ship Channel)

TWDB RECOMMENDED SALTWATER PLANTS

Note: Due to the increasing demand for water, as well as the state's vulnerability to drought events, in 2002 the TWDB undertook the evaluation of 13 proposed large-scale demonstration seawater desalination projects. The TWDB recommended 3 potential projects to proceed to implementation.

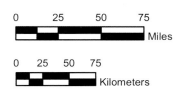
0 25 50 75 Miles

0 25 50 75 Kilometers

Sources: Bureau of Economic Geology, 2004; Texas Water Development Board, 2002.

Groundwater Vulnerability, 2002

Note: The National Water Well Association and the Robert S. Kerr Environmental Research Laboratory developed a method for aquifer vulnerability ranking. Seven parameters assess groundwater pollution potential: annual recharge, aquifer media, soil media, topography, vadose, zone impact, and hydraulic conductivity. "Outcrop" means part of the aquifer is exposed; "downdip" means the aquifer is beneath the earth.

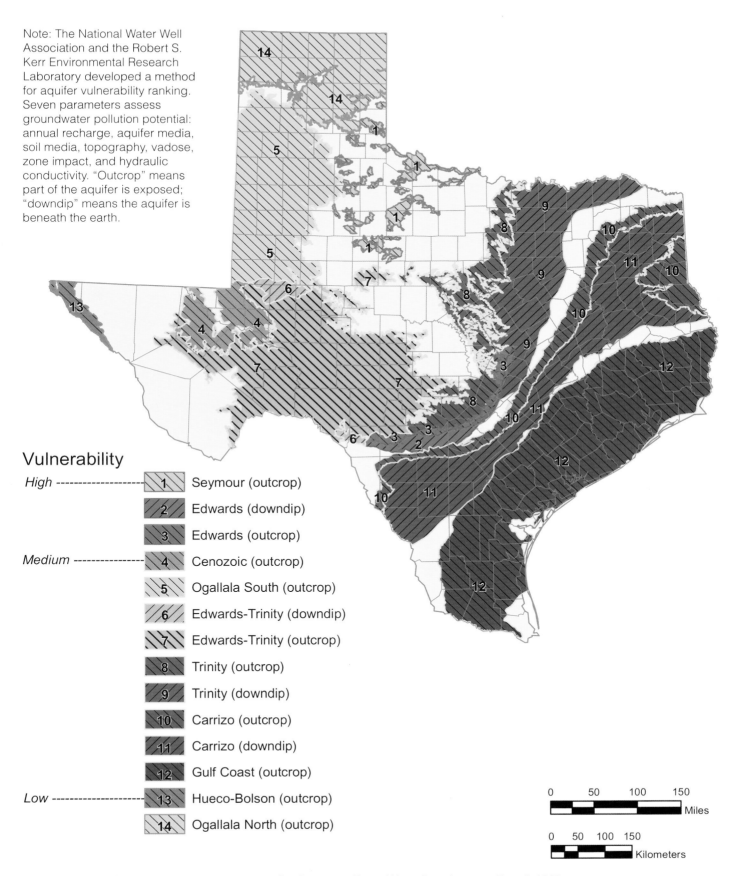

Vulnerability

High -------------------- 1 Seymour (outcrop)

2 Edwards (downdip)

3 Edwards (outcrop)

Medium ---------------- 4 Cenozoic (outcrop)

5 Ogallala South (outcrop)

6 Edwards-Trinity (downdip)

7 Edwards-Trinity (outcrop)

8 Trinity (outcrop)

9 Trinity (downdip)

10 Carrizo (outcrop)

11 Carrizo (downdip)

12 Gulf Coast (outcrop)

Low --------------------- 13 Hueco-Bolson (outcrop)

14 Ogallala North (outcrop)

0   50   100   150
Miles

0   50   100   150
Kilometers

Sources: Texas Commission on Environmental Quality, 2002; Texas Water Development Board, 2002.

Water Wells, 2004
Wells per County

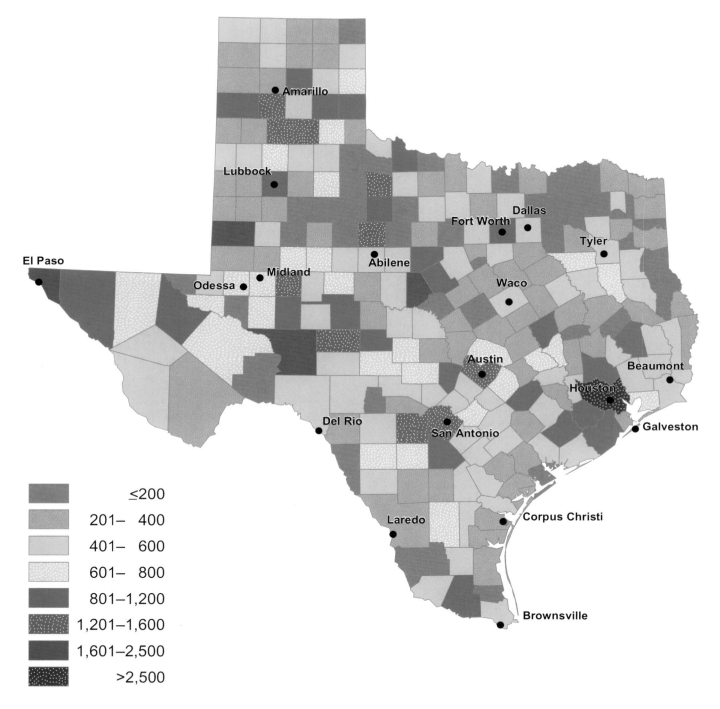

	≤200
	201– 400
	401– 600
	601– 800
	801–1,200
	1,201–1,600
	1,601–2,500
	>2,500

Underground water is located in pervious rocks and soils in either water tables (unconfined) or artesian (confined) aquifers. Texas has 7 major and 16 minor aquifers that provide principal water sources for the state. According to the TWDB, there are 129,491 registered wells in the state. In 1990 groundwater composed over half of the water used in Texas. Groundwater is used for agricultural (71 percent), municipal (21 percent), and industrial (7 percent) purposes.

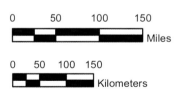

Sources: Texas Water Development Board, 2004; Texas State Historical Association, *Handbook of Texas Online,* 2004.

Water Wells Drilled, 1820–2003

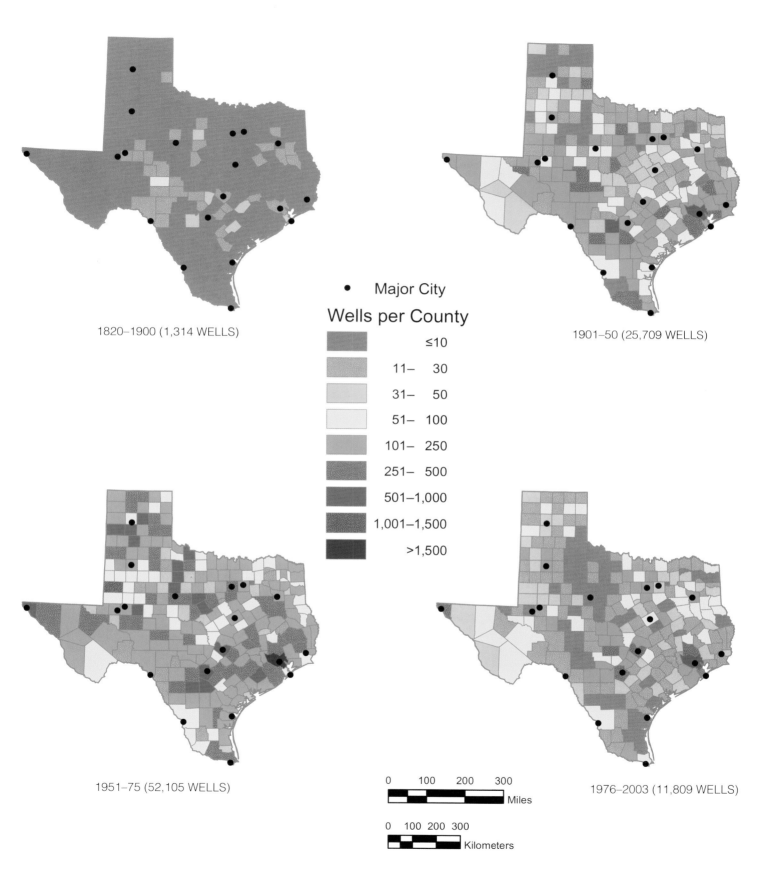

1820–1900 (1,314 WELLS)

1901–50 (25,709 WELLS)

1951–75 (52,105 WELLS)

1976–2003 (11,809 WELLS)

● Major City

Wells per County

≤10
11– 30
31– 50
51– 100
101– 250
251– 500
501–1,000
1,001–1,500
>1,500

0 100 200 300
Miles

0 100 200 300
Kilometers

Source: Texas Water Development Board, 2004.

Water Wells Drilled Annually, 1820–2003

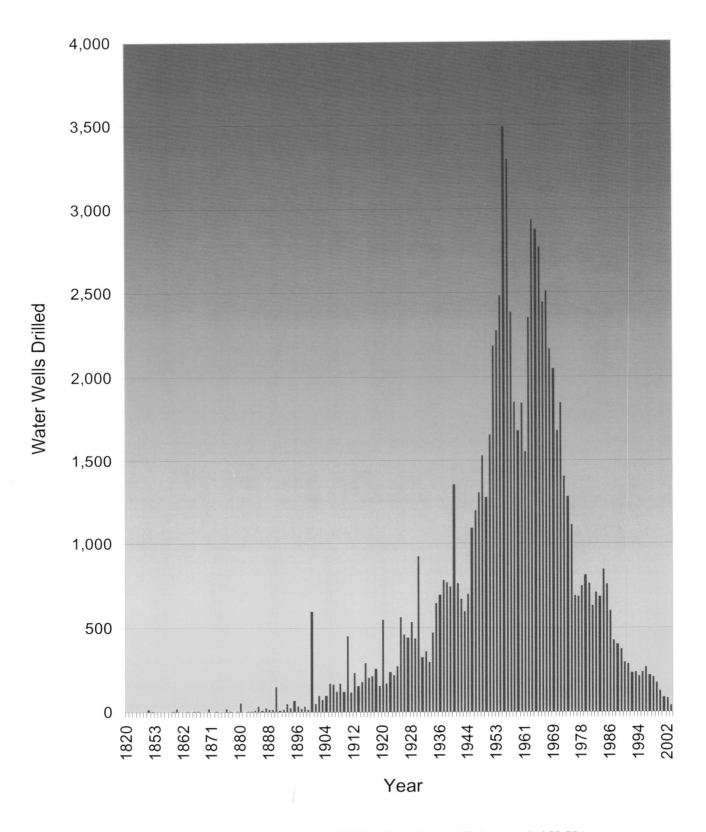

Note: Wells with drill dates and included in graph totaled 90,937. Wells without drill dates totaled 38,554.

Source: Texas Water Development Board, 2004.

Population and Precipitation, 2000

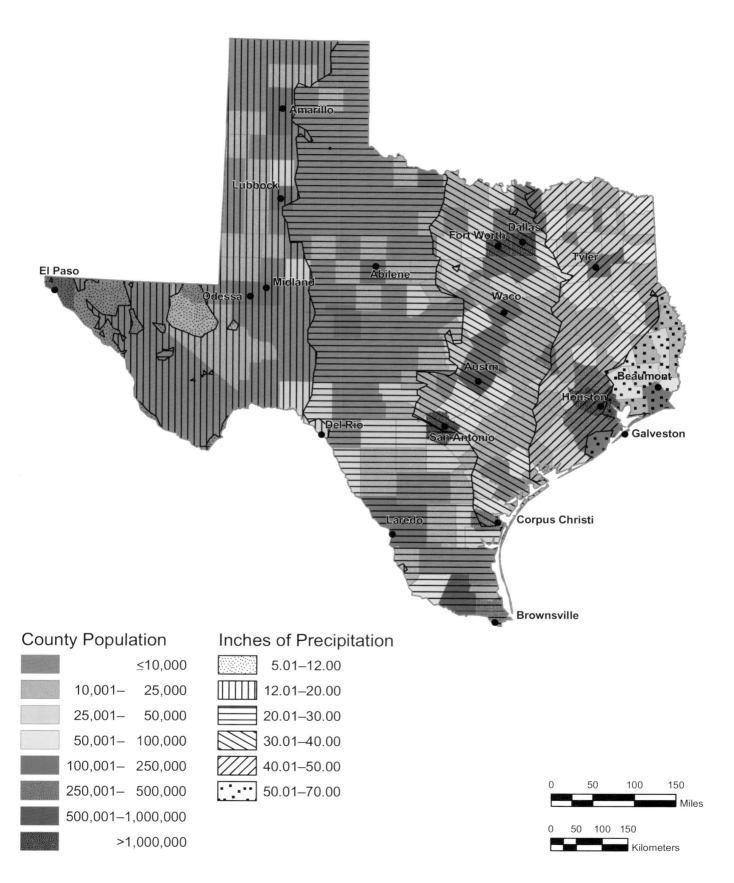

County Population

	≤10,000
	10,001– 25,000
	25,001– 50,000
	50,001– 100,000
	100,001– 250,000
	250,001– 500,000
	500,001–1,000,000
	>1,000,000

Inches of Precipitation

	5.01–12.00
	12.01–20.00
	20.01–30.00
	30.01–40.00
	40.01–50.00
	50.01–70.00

Sources: National Climate Data Center, 2000; U.S. Census Bureau, 2000.

Population and Water Usage, 2003

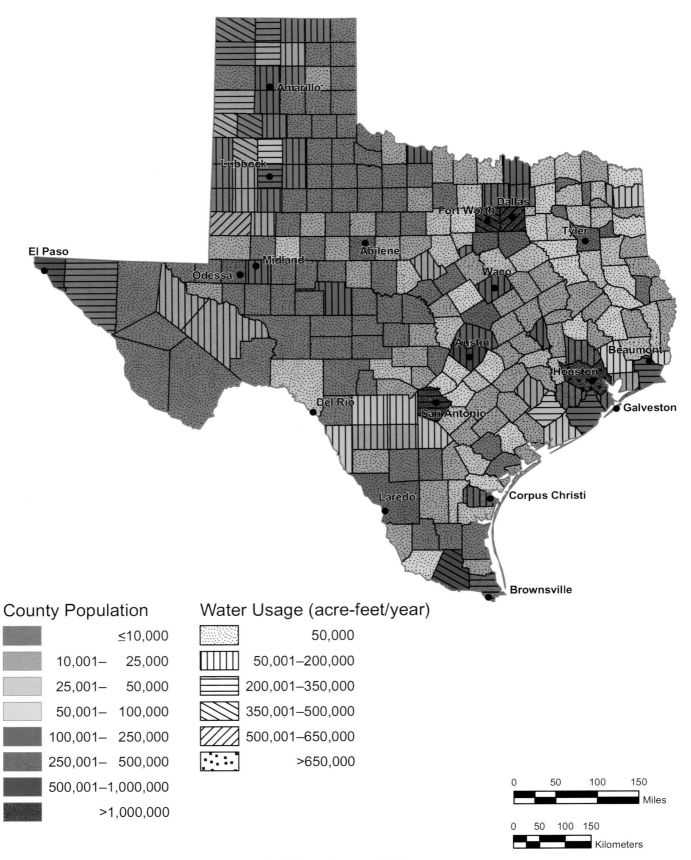

County Population

	≤10,000
	10,001– 25,000
	25,001– 50,000
	50,001– 100,000
	100,001– 250,000
	250,001– 500,000
	500,001–1,000,000
	>1,000,000

Water Usage (acre-feet/year)

	50,000
	50,001–200,000
	200,001–350,000
	350,001–500,000
	500,001–650,000
	>650,000

0   50   100   150
Miles

0   50   100   150
Kilometers

Sources: Texas Water Development Board, 2003; U.S. Census Bureau, 2000.

Water Usage, 2003
Irrigation, Manufacturing, Municipal

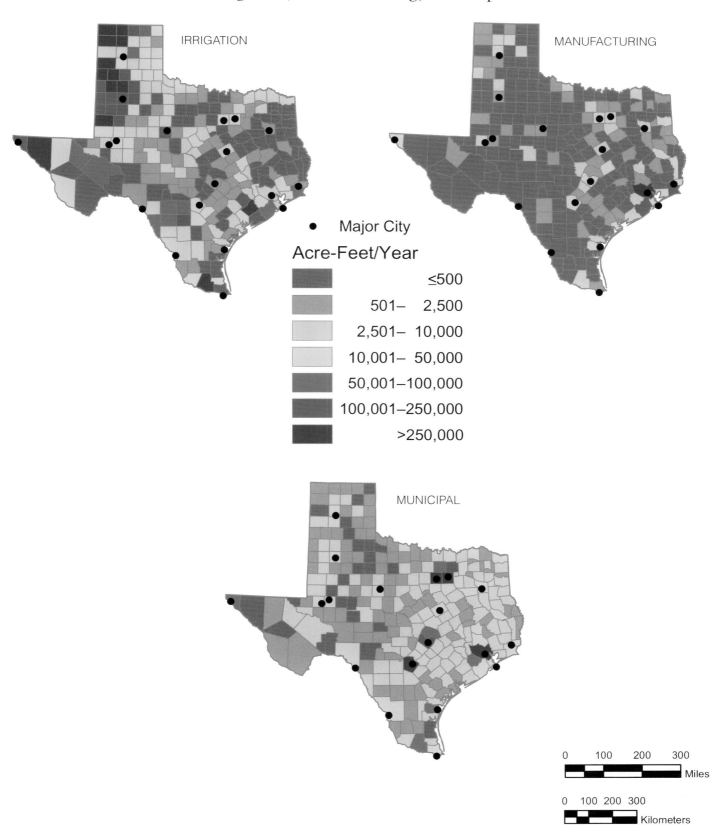

IRRIGATION

MANUFACTURING

MUNICIPAL

● Major City

Acre-Feet/Year

	≤500
	501– 2,500
	2,501– 10,000
	10,001– 50,000
	50,001–100,000
	100,001–250,000
	>250,000

0 100 200 300
Miles

0 100 200 300
Kilometers

Source: Texas Water Development Board, 2003.

Water Usage, 2003
Mining, Livestock, Steam and Electric Production

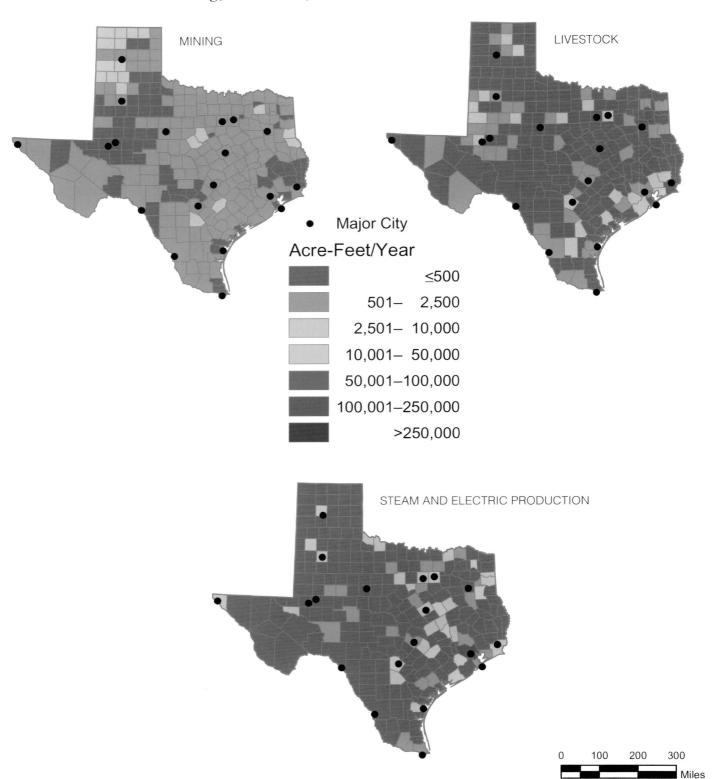

MINING

LIVESTOCK

STEAM AND ELECTRIC PRODUCTION

● Major City

Acre-Feet/Year

	≤500
	501– 2,500
	2,501– 10,000
	10,001– 50,000
	50,001–100,000
	100,001–250,000
	>250,000

0   100   200   300
Miles

0   100 200 300
Kilometers

Source: Texas Water Development Board, 2003.

River Authorities, 2000

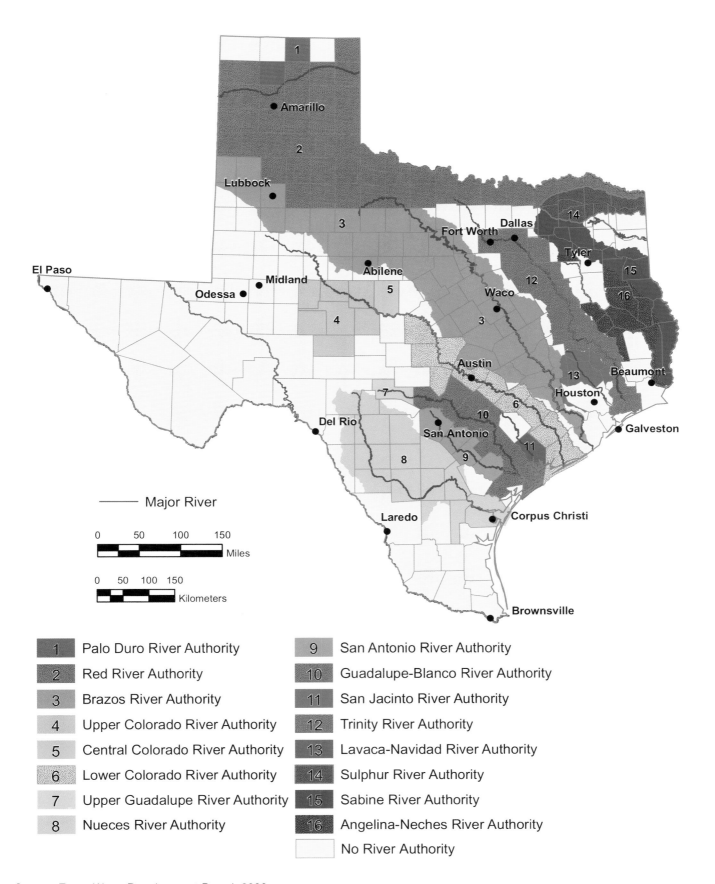

Major River

0 50 100 150
Miles

0 50 100 150
Kilometers

1 Palo Duro River Authority	**9** San Antonio River Authority
2 Red River Authority	**10** Guadalupe-Blanco River Authority
3 Brazos River Authority	**11** San Jacinto River Authority
4 Upper Colorado River Authority	**12** Trinity River Authority
5 Central Colorado River Authority	**13** Lavaca-Navidad River Authority
6 Lower Colorado River Authority	**14** Sulphur River Authority
7 Upper Guadalupe River Authority	**15** Sabine River Authority
8 Nueces River Authority	**16** Angelina-Neches River Authority
	No River Authority

Source: Texas Water Development Board, 2000.

Water Management Regions, 2003
Senate Bill 1 (1997)

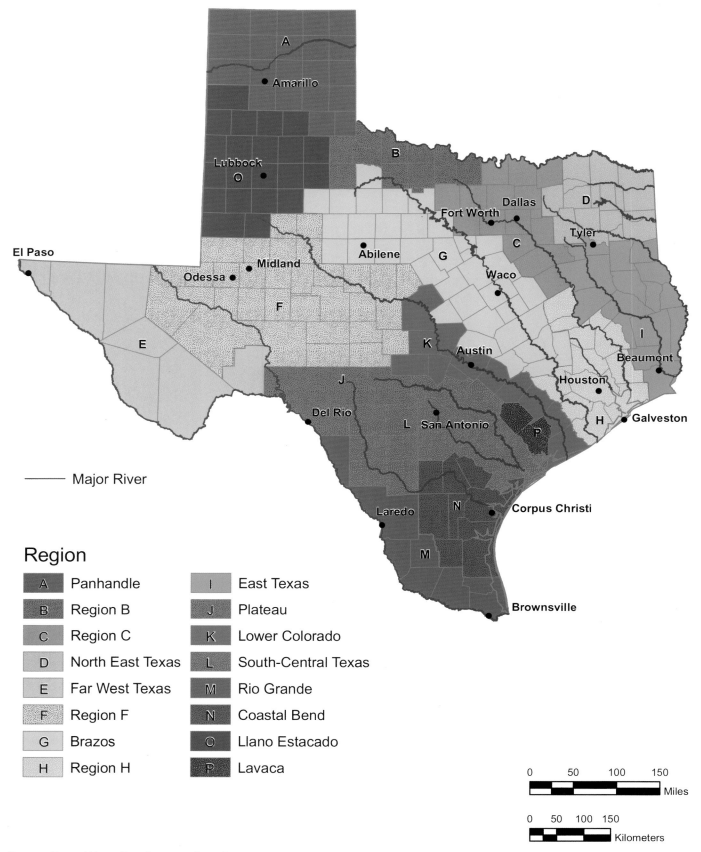

—— Major River

Region

A	Panhandle	I	East Texas
B	Region B	J	Plateau
C	Region C	K	Lower Colorado
D	North East Texas	L	South-Central Texas
E	Far West Texas	M	Rio Grande
F	Region F	N	Coastal Bend
G	Brazos	O	Llano Estacado
H	Region H	P	Lavaca

0   50   100   150
Miles

0   50   100   150
Kilometers

Source: Texas Water Development Board, 2003.

Groundwater Conservation Districts (GCDs)

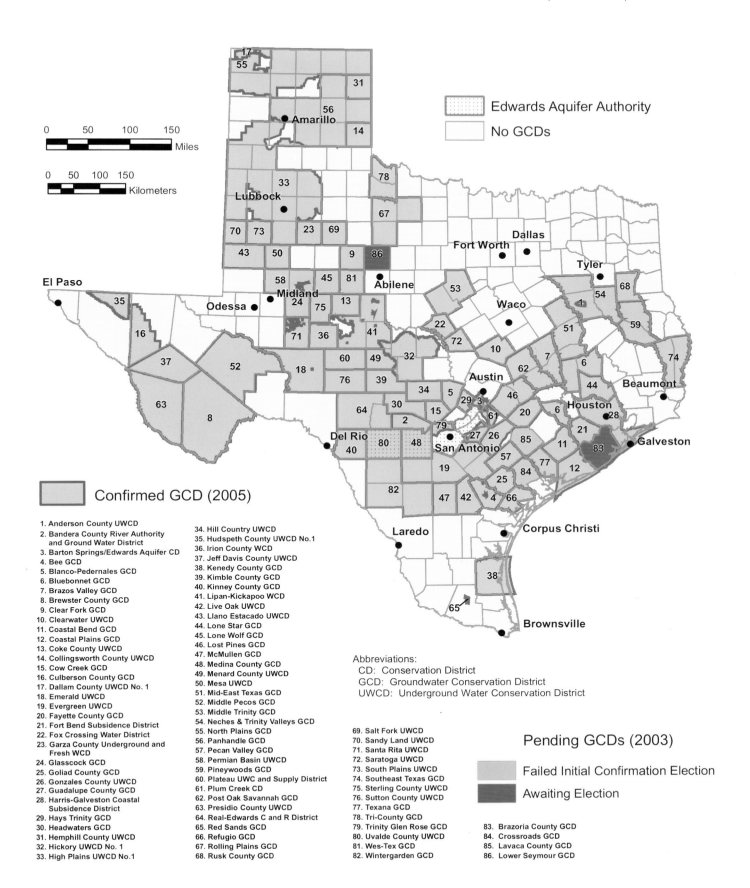

Edwards Aquifer Authority

No GCDs

Confirmed GCD (2005)

1. Anderson County UWCD
2. Bandera County River Authority and Ground Water District
3. Barton Springs/Edwards Aquifer CD
4. Bee GCD
5. Blanco-Pernales GCD
6. Bluebonnet GCD
7. Brazos Valley GCD
8. Brewster County GCD
9. Clear Fork GCD
10. Clearwater UWCD
11. Coastal Bend GCD
12. Coastal Plains GCD
13. Coke County UWCD
14. Collingsworth County UWCD
15. Cow Creek GCD
16. Culberson County GCD
17. Dallam County UWCD No. 1
18. Emerald UWCD
19. Evergreen UWCD
20. Fayette County GCD
21. Fort Bend Subsidence District
22. Fox Crossing Water District
23. Garza County Underground and Fresh WCD
24. Glasscock GCD
25. Goliad County GCD
26. Gonzales County UWCD
27. Guadalupe County GCD
28. Harris-Galveston Coastal Subsidence District
29. Hays Trinity GCD
30. Headwaters GCD
31. Hemphill County UWCD
32. Hickory UWCD No. 1
33. High Plains UWCD No.1

34. Hill Country UWCD
35. Hudspeth County UWCD No.1
36. Irion County WCD
37. Jeff Davis County UWCD
38. Kenedy County GCD
39. Kimble County GCD
40. Kinney County GCD
41. Lipan-Kickapoo WCD
42. Live Oak UWCD
43. Llano Estacado UWCD
44. Lone Star GCD
45. Lone Wolf GCD
46. Lost Pines GCD
47. McMullen GCD
48. Medina County GCD
49. Menard County UWCD
50. Mesa UWCD
51. Mid-East Texas GCD
52. Middle Pecos GCD
53. Middle Trinity GCD
54. Neches & Trinity Valleys GCD
55. North Plains GCD
56. Panhandle GCD
57. Pecan Valley GCD
58. Permian Basin UWCD
59. Pineywoods GCD
60. Plateau UWC and Supply District
61. Plum Creek CD
62. Post Oak Savannah GCD
63. Presidio County UWCD
64. Real-Edwards C and R District
65. Red Sands GCD
66. Refugio GCD
67. Rolling Plains GCD
68. Rusk County GCD

69. Salt Fork UWCD
70. Sandy Land UWCD
71. Santa Rita UWCD
72. Saratoga UWCD
73. South Plains UWCD
74. Southeast Texas GCD
75. Sterling County UWCD
76. Sutton County UWCD
77. Texana GCD
78. Tri-County GCD
79. Trinity Glen Rose GCD
80. Uvalde County UWCD
81. Wes-Tex GCD
82. Wintergarden GCD

Abbreviations:
 CD: Conservation District
 GCD: Groundwater Conservation District
 UWCD: Underground Water Conservation District

Pending GCDs (2003)

Failed Initial Confirmation Election

Awaiting Election

83. Brazoria County GCD
84. Crossroads GCD
85. Lavaca County GCD
86. Lower Seymour GCD

Source: Texas Water Development Board, 2005.

5

Water Projects, Pollution, and Protection

TEXAS IS NOTABLE FOR THE RELATIVELY modest development of two uses of its surface streams. First, Texas has few streams that are potentially navigable for present-day commerce. The only stream considered for a major modern navigation project was the Trinity River, but the river's channelization was abandoned in 1973 because of soaring costs. Commercial navigation is undertaken in the tidal reaches of the Rio Grande via the Brownsville Ship Channel and the Guadalupe River to Victoria. The Houston Ship Channel provides a route for oceangoing vessels to reach the state's largest port.

Second, Texas lacks significant hydroelectric power. Effective hydroelectric generation requires both substantial discharge and sharp relief. West Texas has considerable relief but little discharge. In contrast, East Texas has ample discharge but little relief. Because of this geographic mismatch, hydropower generates less than 2 percent of all the electricity consumed in the state (USDOE 2006). The largest hydroelectric dams are the Mansfield Dam on the Colorado River at Austin (rated at 102 megawatts) and the Toledo Bend Dam on the Sabine River (83 megawatts), both of which pale in comparison to Hoover Dam (1,700 megawatts) and Grande Coulee Dam (6,400 megawatts) (USDOE 2006).

Until the environmental era of the 1960s and 1970s, there was relatively little concern about water and air pollution (air pollution can affect water bodies negatively through "chemical washout," which increases their acidity) and overall environmental degradation beyond clearly observable health threats and aesthetic apprehension in high-value residential, retail, and recreational areas (Kline 2000). The environment, particularly water quality, paid a high price during the economic growth of Texas. Many streams became devoid of desirable fish, became unsafe for swimming, and contained dangerous concentrations of chemicals hazardous to humans and wildlife. The pollutants responsible for this degradation were either discharged directly into receiving water bodies as "point source" pol-

lution or carried off the land by storm runoff as "nonpoint source" pollution. Point source pollution, responsible for about one-third of the water quality deterioration, was the easiest to regulate and came under the purview of the federal Clean Water Acts of 1972 and 1977. Runoff from the land, nonpoint source pollution, was not significantly regulated until the federal 1987 Water Quality Act established restrictions on urban areas with populations of more than one hundred thousand, construction sites, and concentrated animal feeding operations (CAFOs). Streams that did not meet the "swimmable, fishable, potentially drinkable" standard were placed on the "303d list" as "impaired water bodies," and government funds were made available to reduce the "Total Maximum Daily Load" (TMDL) of the pollutants entering the water bodies (Cech 2005; Houck 1999; Norwine, Giardino, and Kashwamurthy 2005).

Protecting groundwater quality has its own set of unique challenges. Most groundwater contamination comes from the diffuse infiltration of recharged surface waters in a manner analogous to nonpoint source surface pollution. Direct injection of liquid waste disposal and of enhanced oil and gas recovery can cause immediate contamination of aquifers. Limestone aquifers, such as the Edwards and Trinity aquifers, are particularly vulnerable because limestone and other carbonate rocks usually have pore spaces so large that the pollutants are not trapped by the rock particles. Landfills have received special attention because of the contamination threat by their leachate—water that dissolves pollutants and transports them as it percolates through the landfills. To prevent such contamination, the legislature passed strict rules for landfill siting, construction, and monitoring in 1984, resulting in dramatic increases in charges for solid waste disposal and the closing of hundreds of small landfills that could not meet the new standards (TCEQ 2004–2006).

The locations of specific water quality problems reflect the distribution of cities, industry, and agricultural activities. CAFOs and intensive irrigation agriculture have resulted in high levels of nitrogen and phosphorus in the groundwater of the High Plains. Old cities with leaky sewer systems or dense suburban developments with septic systems rather than centralized treatment systems have both bacteriological and nitrogen pollution. Traditional mining activities increase both suspended sediment, which reduces water clarity, and bed loads that contribute to flood hazards. Oil and gas activities have their own special array of problems, ranging from the disposal of brine used to enhance recovery to the release of hydrocarbons that consume oxygen in water bodies or cause health problems. Activities that release heavy metals and other nonsoluble chemicals become more concentrated as they move up the "food chain" and cause disease and birth defects in the "top predators," regardless of whether they are fish, birds, or humans.

Concern about degradation and destruction of wild lands and their fauna has provided additional justification for reducing water pollutants, as well as efforts to protect specific environments and species. For many decades wildlife ecologists and hydrologists have recognized the critical biological and hydrological role performed by wetlands—the shallow, periodically flooded areas adjacent to rivers and coastal bays. This knowledge has taken a long time to enter the realm of public action. Traditional views are that "swamps" are bad and breed disease and that any

freshwater that makes it to the coast is "wasted." Nearly a century of ecological research has shown that wetlands are among the most productive and diverse ecosystems. Coastal wetlands are the "nurseries" of many commercially important marine species, such as crabs, shrimp, and redfish (Kline 2000; Cech 2005; Britton and Morton 1998). Wetlands are so efficient in removing pollutants that many wastewater systems use "constructed" wetlands as a part of their treatment of municipal and agricultural effluent and runoff (Corbitt 1999). However, invasive plant species, such as salt cedar, have pushed up the banks of many Texas streams and consume large amounts of water on a daily basis (TCEQ 2004–2006; Carpenter 1998).

Recognition that "extinction is forever" has prompted the listing of many Texas plants and animals as "endangered" or "threatened." The realization of the necessity to protect physically endangered species and their environments has led to the designation of "critical habitats." Protecting critical habitat has been used to restrict pumping from the Edwards Aquifer, halt commercial and residential developments, and mandate minimum freshwater inflows into coastal bays and estuaries to maintain salinities lower than prescribed levels. Such restrictions have also sparked a political backlash against environmental legislation and have fueled "Take Back Texas" and other antigovernment and antienvironmental legislation (USFWS 2006).

National Waterway Network in Texas, 2001

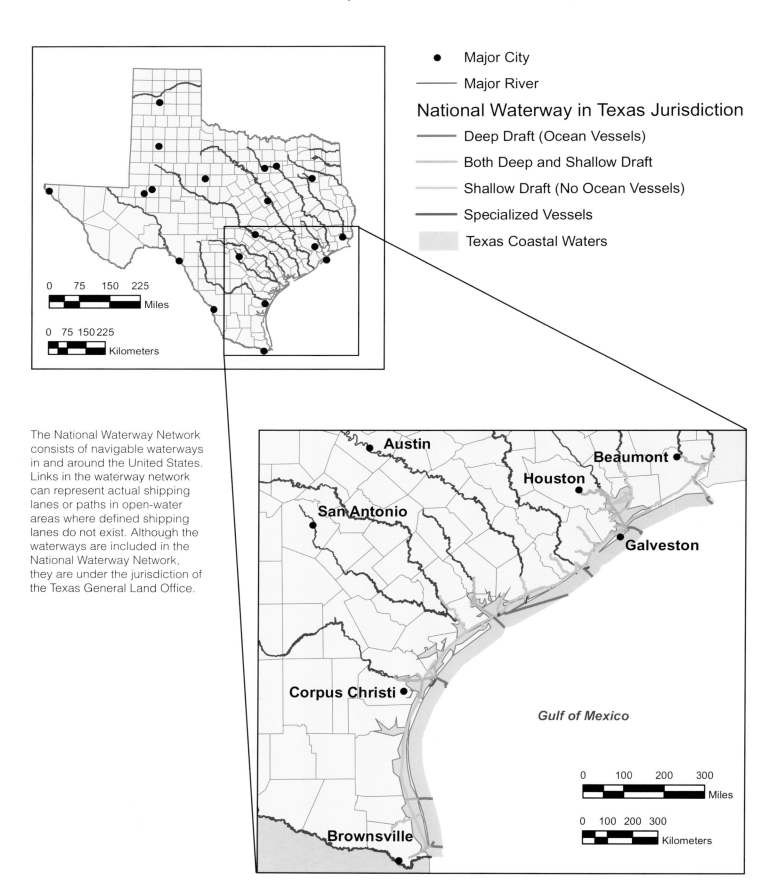

Major City

Major River

National Waterway in Texas Jurisdiction

Deep Draft (Ocean Vessels)

Both Deep and Shallow Draft

Shallow Draft (No Ocean Vessels)

Specialized Vessels

Texas Coastal Waters

0 75 150 225 Miles

0 75 150 225 Kilometers

The National Waterway Network consists of navigable waterways in and around the United States. Links in the waterway network can represent actual shipping lanes or paths in open-water areas where defined shipping lanes do not exist. Although the waterways are included in the National Waterway Network, they are under the jurisdiction of the Texas General Land Office.

Austin

Beaumont

Houston

San Antonio

Galveston

Corpus Christi

Gulf of Mexico

0 100 200 300 Miles

0 100 200 300 Kilometers

Brownsville

Source: U.S. Bureau of Transportation Statistics, 2001.

Hydroelectric Power, 1999

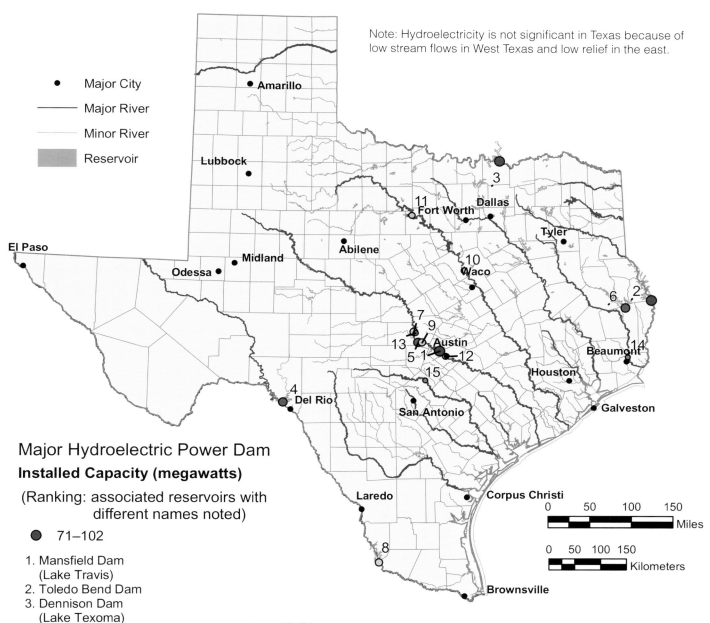

Note: Hydroelectricity is not significant in Texas because of low stream flows in West Texas and low relief in the east.

Legend:
- ● Major City
- —— Major River
- —— Minor River
- ▓ Reservoir

Major Hydroelectric Power Dam

Installed Capacity (megawatts)

(Ranking: associated reservoirs with different names noted)

● 71–102

1. Mansfield Dam (Lake Travis)
2. Toledo Bend Dam
3. Dennison Dam (Lake Texoma)

● 52–70

4. International Amistad Dam
5. Alvin Wirtz Dam (Lake Lyndon B. Johnson)
6. Sam Rayburn Dam

◎ 31–51

7. Buchanan Dam
8. International Falcon Lake Dam
9. Max Starcke Dam (Lake Marble Falls)

○ 16–30

10. Whitney Dam
11. Morris Sheppard Dam (Possum Kingdom Lake)
12. Tom Miller Dam (Lake Austin)

◦ 6–15

13. Inks Dam
14. Town Bluff Dam (B. S. Steinhagen Lake)
15. Canyon Dam

Mansfield Dam on Lake Travis. Photo by Lower Colorado River Authority, 2006.

Sources: U.S. Geological Survey, 1999; Texas Water Development Board, 1999.

5.3. MAJOR TEXAS HYDROELECTRIC PLANTS, 2005

Rank by U.S. Capacity	Dam	Reservoir	River	Installed Capacity (megawatts)	Operator
1	Mansfield	Lake Travis	Colorado	102	Lower Colorado River Authority
2	Toledo Bend	Toledo Bend	Sabine	83	Sabine River Authority
3	Dennison	Lake Texoma	Red	80	U.S. Army Corps of Engineers
4	Amistad	International Amistad	Rio Grande	70 U.S.; 33 Mexico	International Boundary and Water Commission
5	Alvin Wirtz	Lake LBJ	Colorado	56	Lower Colorado River Authority
6	Sam Rayburn	Sam Rayburn	Angelina	52	U.S. Army Corps of Engineers
7	Buchanan	Lake Buchanan	Colorado	51	Lower Colorado River Authority
8	Falcon	International Falcon	Rio Grande	39 U.S.; 31.5 Mexico	International Boundary and Water Commission
9	Max Starcke	Lake Marble Falls	Colorado	32	Lower Colorado River Authority
10	Whitney	Whitney	Brazos	30	U.S. Army Corps of Engineers
11	Morris Sheppard	Possum Kingdom Lake	Brazos	25	Brazos River Authority
12	Tom Miller	Lake Austin	Colorado	17	Lower Colorado River Authority
13	Inks	Inks Lake	Colorado	14	Lower Colorado River Authority
14	Town Bluff	B. A. Steinhagen Lake	Neches	8	U.S. Army Corps of Engineers
15	Canyon	Canyon Lake	Guadalupe	6	Guadalupe-Blanco River Authority

Sources: Energy Information Administration, 2005; Texas Public Utility Commission, 2005; operators of individual hydroelectric plants, 2005.

Note: Minor discrepancies are due to different values provided by different sources for the same dam.

Oil and Natural Gas Production, 2003

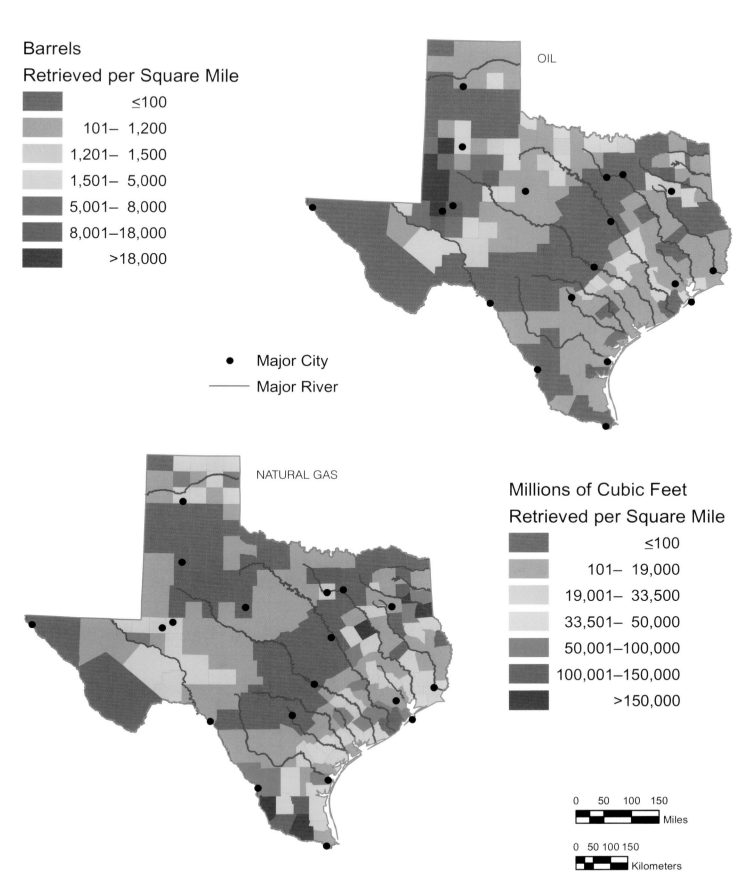

Barrels
Retrieved per Square Mile

- ≤100
- 101– 1,200
- 1,201– 1,500
- 1,501– 5,000
- 5,001– 8,000
- 8,001–18,000
- >18,000

OIL

- Major City
- Major River

NATURAL GAS

Millions of Cubic Feet
Retrieved per Square Mile

- ≤100
- 101– 19,000
- 19,001– 33,500
- 33,501– 50,000
- 50,001–100,000
- 100,001–150,000
- >150,000

0   50   100   150
Miles

0 50 100 150
Kilometers

Source: Railroad Commission of Texas, 2003.

Industrial Pollutants
Leaking Underground Tanks, 2001, and Industrial Hazardous Waste, 1997

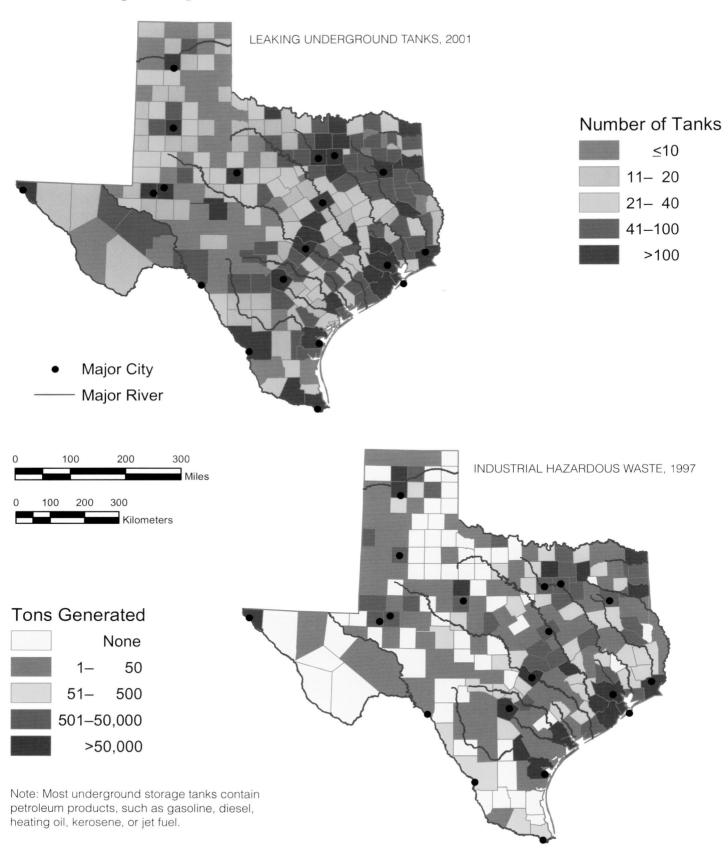

LEAKING UNDERGROUND TANKS, 2001

Number of Tanks

≤10
11– 20
21– 40
41–100
>100

● Major City

— Major River

0   100   200   300
Miles

0   100   200   300
Kilometers

Tons Generated

None
1–   50
51–   500
501–50,000
>50,000

Note: Most underground storage tanks contain petroleum products, such as gasoline, diesel, heating oil, kerosene, or jet fuel.

INDUSTRIAL HAZARDOUS WASTE, 1997

Source: Texas Environmental Profiles, 2004.

Industrial Pollutants, 2004
Mining Operations and Nuclear or Radioactive

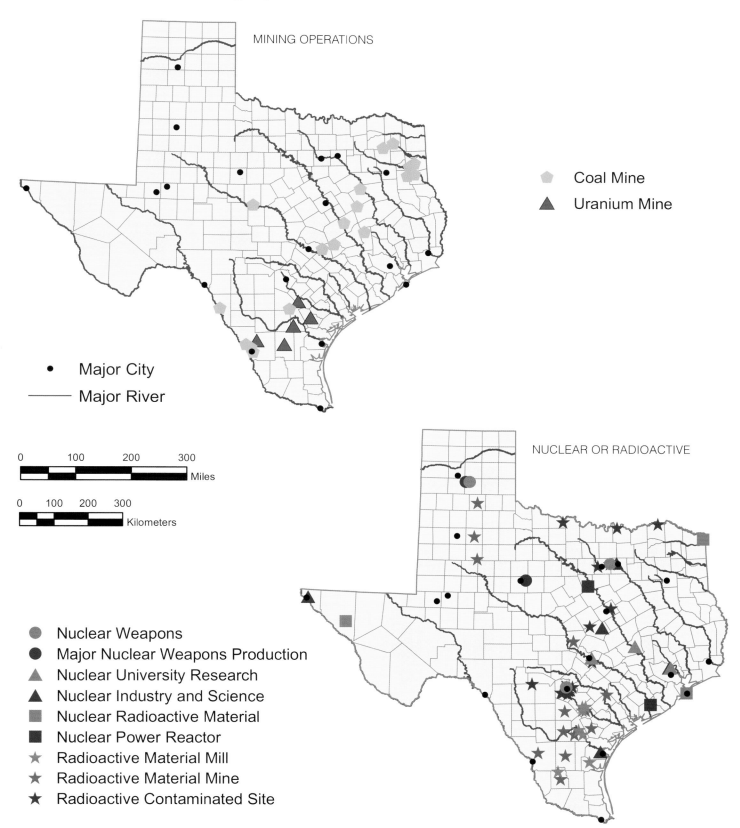

MINING OPERATIONS

Coal Mine

Uranium Mine

• Major City

— Major River

0   100   200   300
Miles

0   100   200   300
Kilometers

NUCLEAR OR RADIOACTIVE

Nuclear Weapons
Major Nuclear Weapons Production
Nuclear University Research
Nuclear Industry and Science
Nuclear Radioactive Material
Nuclear Power Reactor
Radioactive Material Mill
Radioactive Material Mine
Radioactive Contaminated Site

Sources: Railroad Commission of Texas, 2004; WISE Uranium Project, 2004.

Agricultural Pollutants, 2004
Animal Waste and Groundwater Contamination

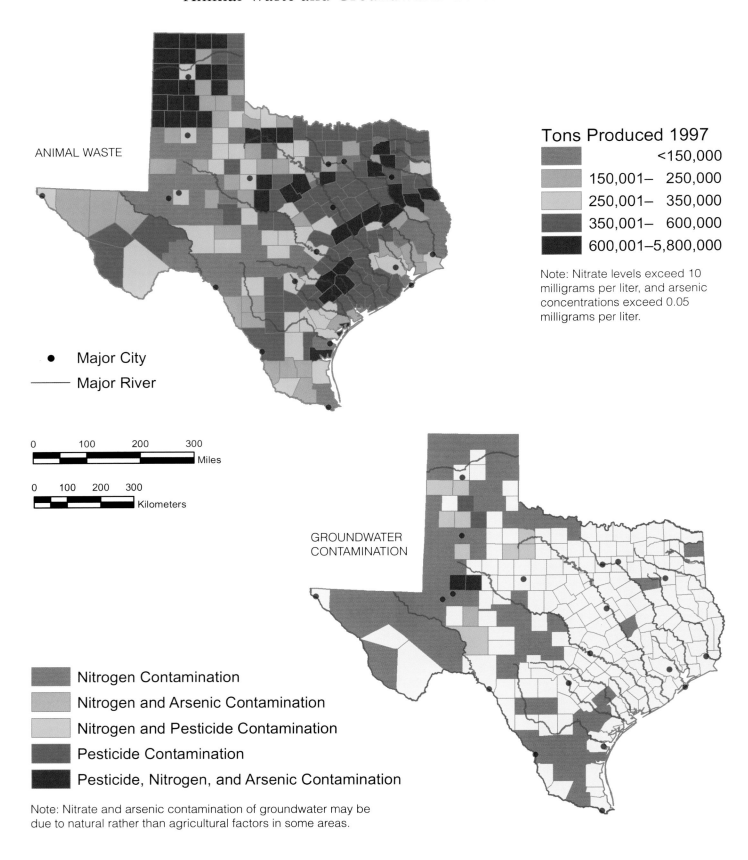

ANIMAL WASTE

Tons Produced 1997

	<150,000
	150,001– 250,000
	250,001– 350,000
	350,001– 600,000
	600,001–5,800,000

Note: Nitrate levels exceed 10 milligrams per liter, and arsenic concentrations exceed 0.05 milligrams per liter.

● Major City

— Major River

```
0    100   200   300
                        Miles

0   100  200  300
                    Kilometers
```

GROUNDWATER CONTAMINATION

Nitrogen Contamination

Nitrogen and Arsenic Contamination

Nitrogen and Pesticide Contamination

Pesticide Contamination

Pesticide, Nitrogen, and Arsenic Contamination

Note: Nitrate and arsenic contamination of groundwater may be due to natural rather than agricultural factors in some areas.

Source: Texas Environmental Profiles, 2004.

Concentrated Animal Feeding Operations (CAFOs)

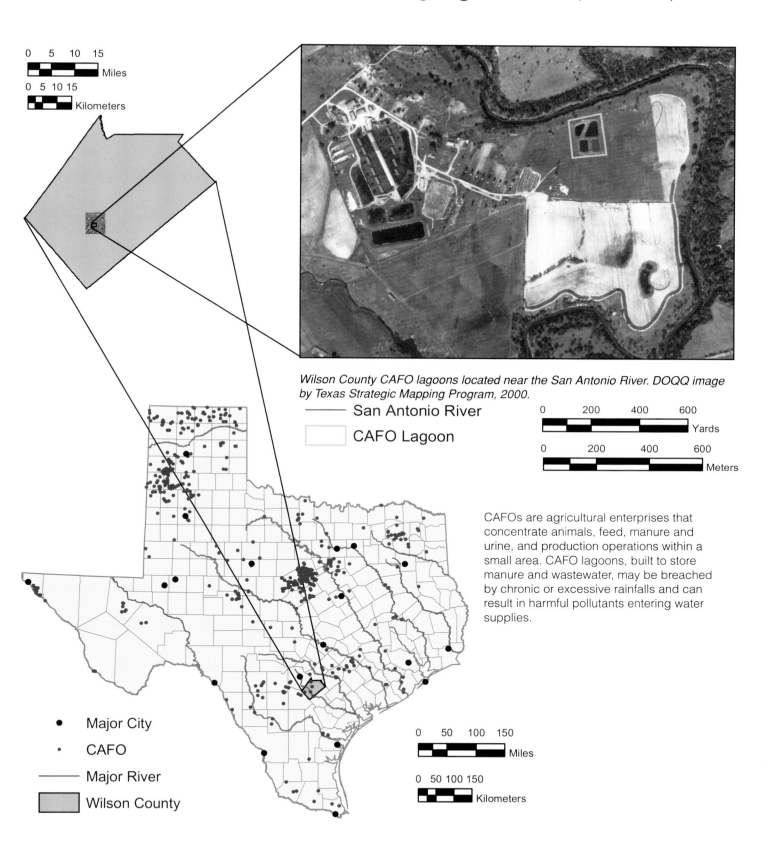

0 5 10 15 Miles

0 5 10 15 Kilometers

Wilson County CAFO lagoons located near the San Antonio River. DOQQ image by Texas Strategic Mapping Program, 2000.

———— San Antonio River

☐ CAFO Lagoon

0   200   400   600 Yards

0   200   400   600 Meters

CAFOs are agricultural enterprises that concentrate animals, feed, manure and urine, and production operations within a small area. CAFO lagoons, built to store manure and wastewater, may be breached by chronic or excessive rainfalls and can result in harmful pollutants entering water supplies.

● Major City

· CAFO

—— Major River

▨ Wilson County

0   50   100   150 Miles

0 50 100 150 Kilometers

Sources: Texas Natural Resource Conservation Commission, 2001; U.S. Environmental Protection Agency, 2003; Texas Strategic Mapping Program, 2006.

Sanitary Landfills
Number of People Served, 1996

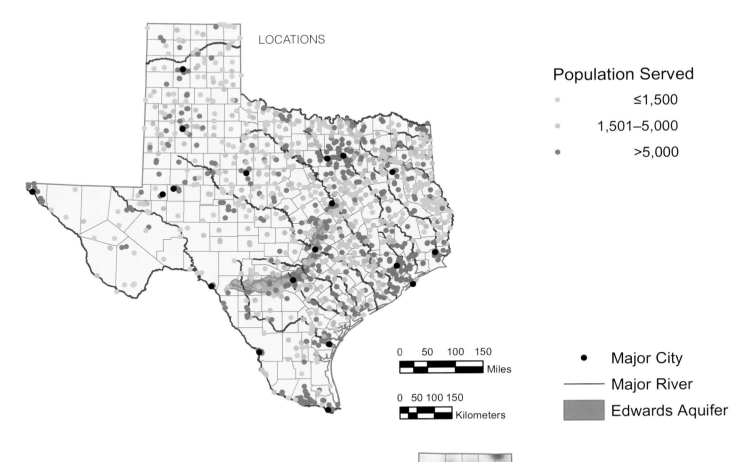

LOCATIONS

Population Served

≤1,500

1,501–5,000

>5,000

0   50   100   150
Miles

0   50 100 150
Kilometers

● Major City

—— Major River

▨ Edwards Aquifer

A sanitary landfill is an engineered site for disposing of solid waste on land in such a way that hazards to health and safety are reduced. Methods include the use of clay or synthetic liners and the control of water drainage to confine the landfill waste to the smallest practical volume. In addition, sanitary landfills have environmental monitoring systems, leachate collection systems, and methane gas controls. Heavy equipment is used to spread, compact, and cover the refuse daily with a minimum of 6 inches of compacted dirt. Following the attainment of maximum capacity, a landfill is covered with a 2- or 3-foot-thick top layer of dirt and vegetation.

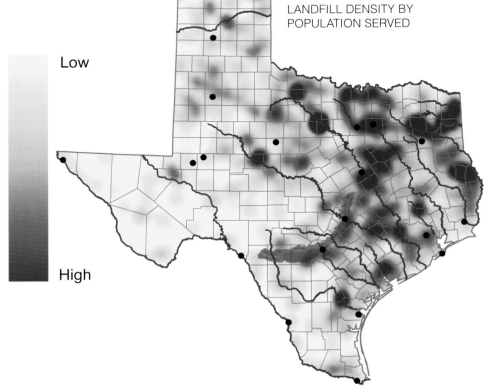

Low

High

LANDFILL DENSITY BY
POPULATION SERVED

Source: Texas Natural Resources Information System, 1996.

Landfills
Other Attributes, 1996

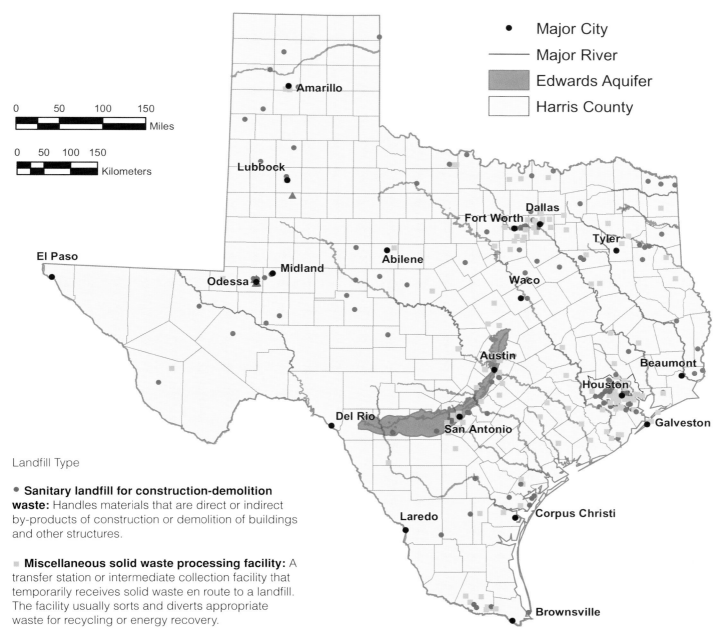

Major City •
Major River —
Edwards Aquifer
Harris County

Amarillo
Lubbock
Dallas
Fort Worth
Tyler
El Paso
Abilene
Midland
Odessa
Waco
Austin
Beaumont
Houston
Del Rio
San Antonio
Galveston
Laredo
Corpus Christi
Brownsville

Landfill Type

● **Sanitary landfill for construction-demolition waste:** Handles materials that are direct or indirect by-products of construction or demolition of buildings and other structures.

▪ **Miscellaneous solid waste processing facility:** A transfer station or intermediate collection facility that temporarily receives solid waste en route to a landfill. The facility usually sorts and diverts appropriate waste for recycling or energy recovery.

▲ **Experimental facilities:** Includes those that operate under a new proposed method of managing municipal solid waste. These methods can include resource and energy recovery projects.

⬠ **Methane gas recovery:** Usually takes place on inactive landfills. Methane is a naturally occurring by-product of landfills produced by decomposing materials. Recovered gas can be used a fuel source.

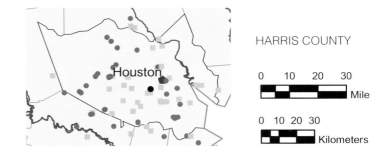

HARRIS COUNTY

Houston

Source: Texas Natural Resources Information System, 1996.

Facilities Emitting Air Pollutants, 1999

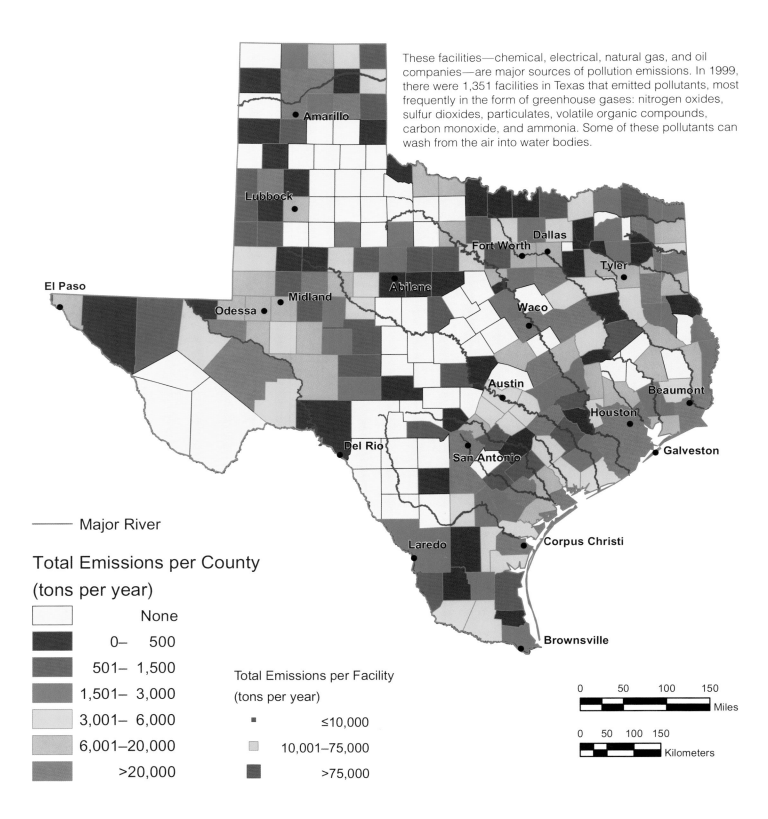

These facilities—chemical, electrical, natural gas, and oil companies—are major sources of pollution emissions. In 1999, there were 1,351 facilities in Texas that emitted pollutants, most frequently in the form of greenhouse gases: nitrogen oxides, sulfur dioxides, particulates, volatile organic compounds, carbon monoxide, and ammonia. Some of these pollutants can wash from the air into water bodies.

—— Major River

Total Emissions per County
(tons per year)

	None
	0– 500
	501– 1,500
	1,501– 3,000
	3,001– 6,000
	6,001–20,000
	>20,000

Total Emissions per Facility
(tons per year)

■	≤10,000
	10,001–75,000
	>75,000

0   50   100   150
Miles

0 50 100 150
Kilometers

Source: U.S. Environmental Protection Agency, 1999.

Wastewater Discharge, 2002

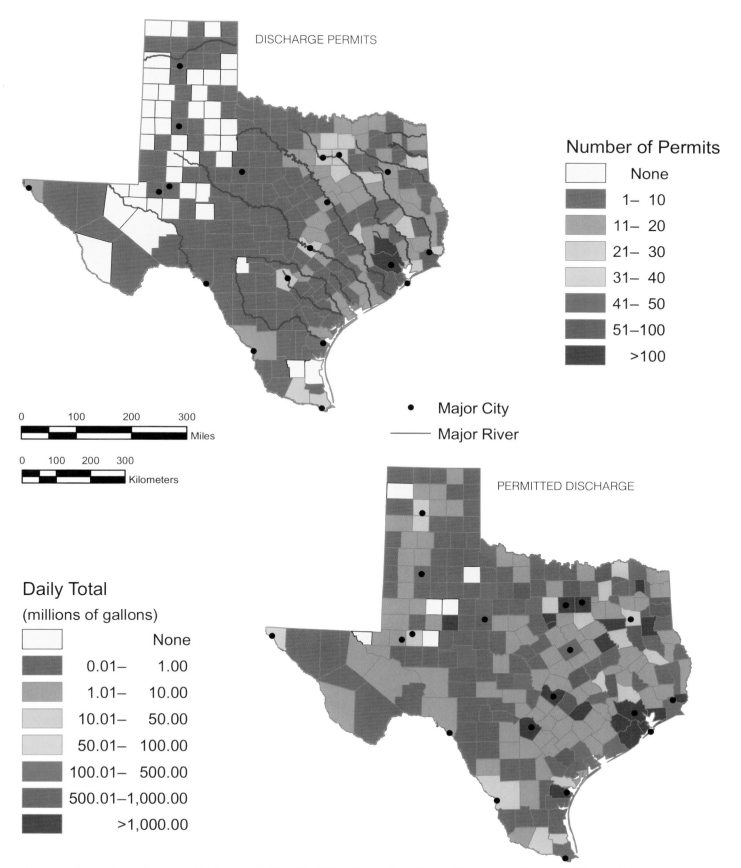

DISCHARGE PERMITS

Number of Permits

	None
	1– 10
	11– 20
	21– 30
	31– 40
	41– 50
	51–100
	>100

• Major City

— Major River

PERMITTED DISCHARGE

0 100 200 300 Miles

0 100 200 300 Kilometers

Daily Total

(millions of gallons)

	None
0.01–	1.00
1.01–	10.00
10.01–	50.00
50.01–	100.00
100.01–	500.00
500.01–	1,000.00
	>1,000.00

Sources: Texas Commission on Environmental Quality, 2004; City of San Marcos Wastewater Treatment Plant, 2006.

Toxic Substances in Surface Waters, 1999

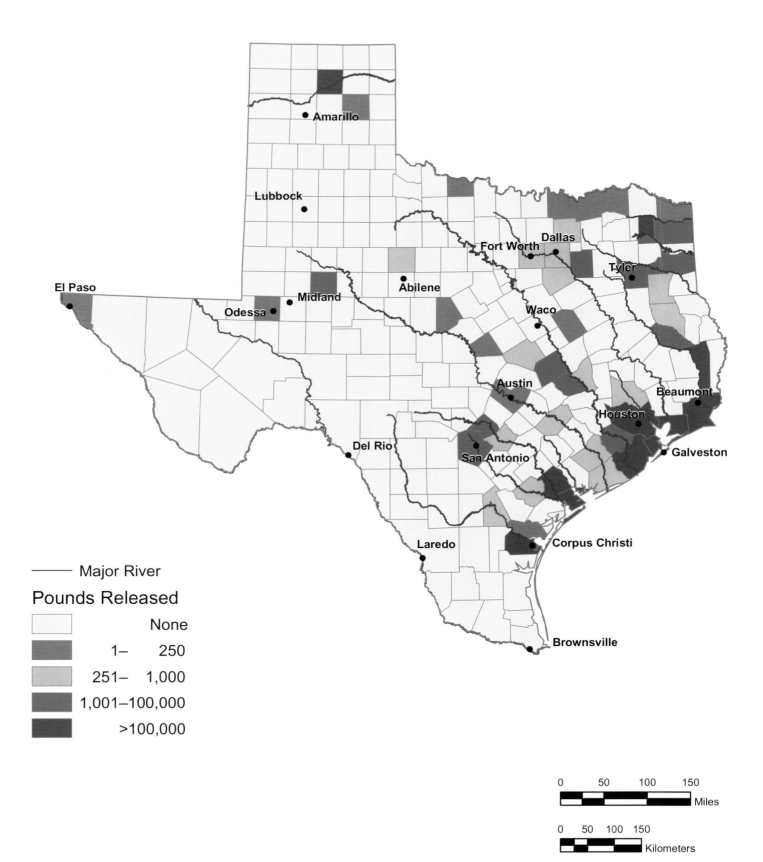

Major River

Pounds Released

	None
	1– 250
	251– 1,000
	1,001–100,000
	>100,000

0   50   100   150
Miles

0   50   100   150
Kilometers

Source: Texas Environmental Profiles, 2004.

Locations of Fish Kills, 1958–2005

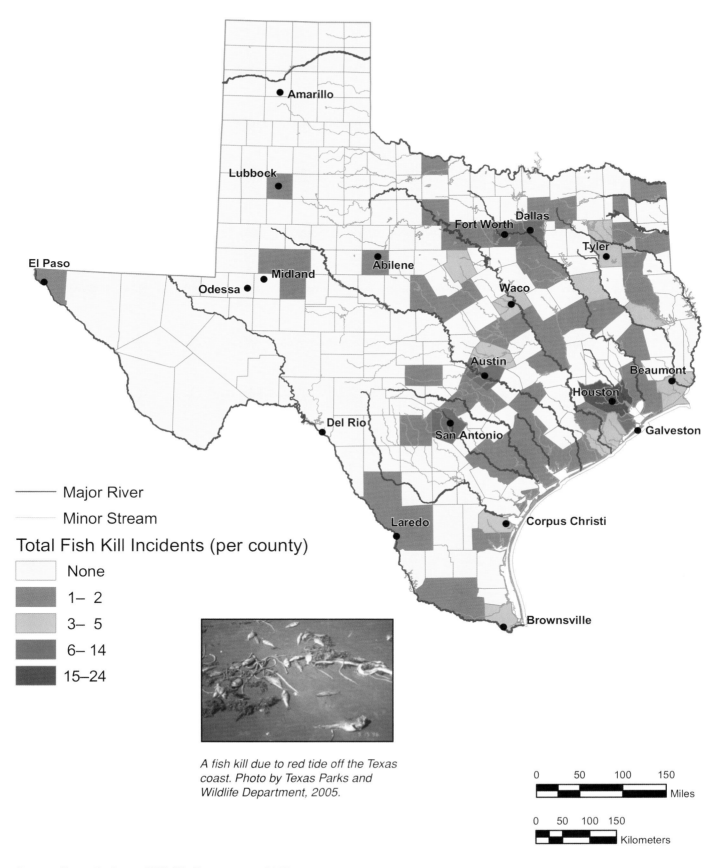

Major River

Minor Stream

Total Fish Kill Incidents (per county)

- None
- 1– 2
- 3– 5
- 6– 14
- 15–24

El Paso

Amarillo

Lubbock

Midland

Odessa

Abilene

Fort Worth

Dallas

Tyler

Waco

Austin

Beaumont

Houston

San Antonio

Galveston

Del Rio

Laredo

Corpus Christi

Brownsville

A fish kill due to red tide off the Texas coast. Photo by Texas Parks and Wildlife Department, 2005.

0   50   100   150
Miles

0   50 100 150
Kilometers

Source: Texas Parks and Wildlife Department, 2005.

Endangered Water-Dependent Species, 2004
Fish, Mammals, and Birds

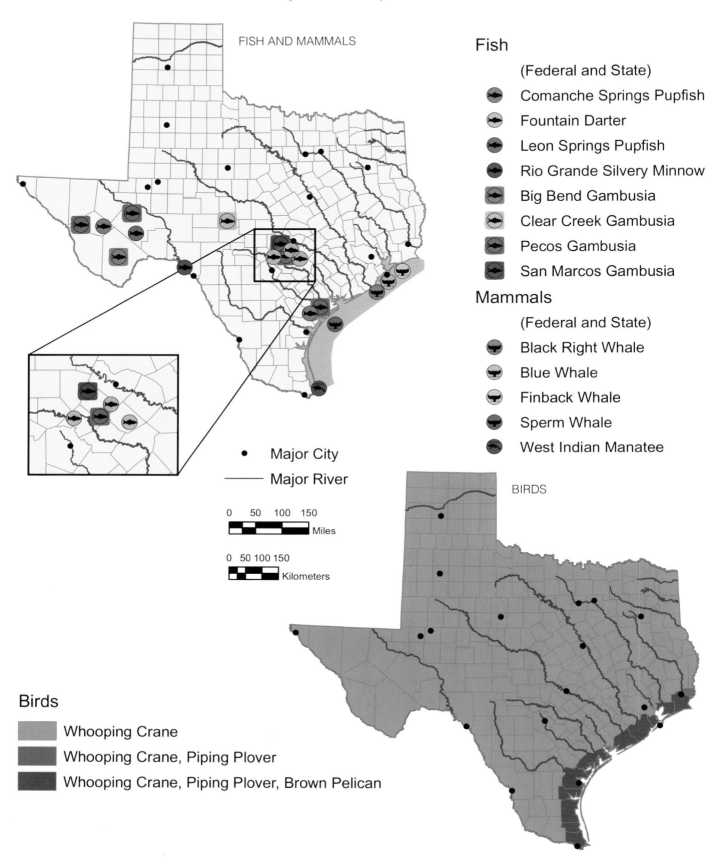

FISH AND MAMMALS

Fish

(Federal and State)

- Comanche Springs Pupfish
- Fountain Darter
- Leon Springs Pupfish
- Rio Grande Silvery Minnow
- Big Bend Gambusia
- Clear Creek Gambusia
- Pecos Gambusia
- San Marcos Gambusia

Mammals

(Federal and State)

- Black Right Whale
- Blue Whale
- Finback Whale
- Sperm Whale
- West Indian Manatee

● Major City

— Major River

0   50   100   150
Miles

0   50 100 150
Kilometers

BIRDS

Birds

Whooping Crane

Whooping Crane, Piping Plover

Whooping Crane, Piping Plover, Brown Pelican

Source: Texas Parks and Wildlife Department, 2004.

Endangered Water-Dependent Species, 2004
Other Animals and Plants

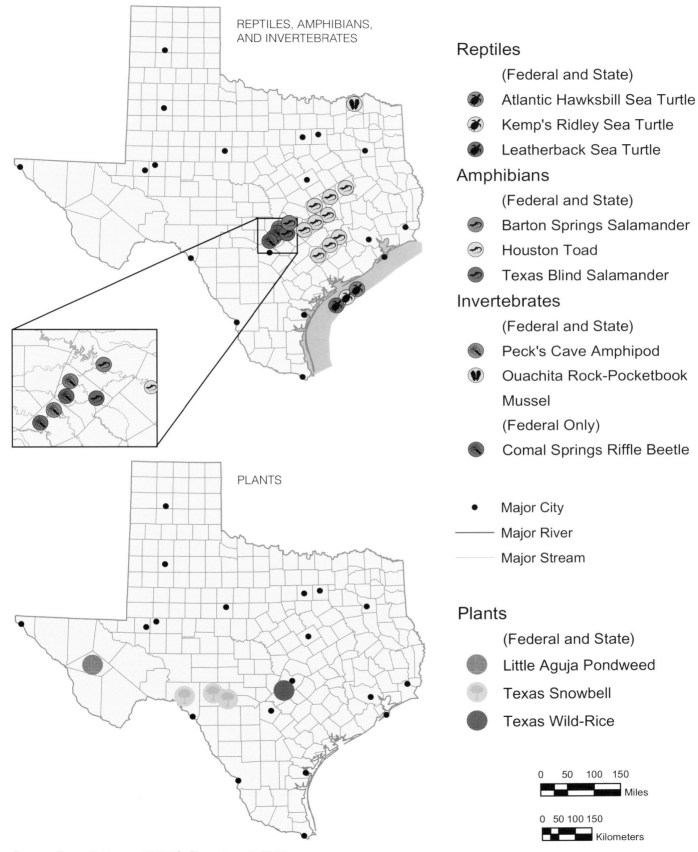

REPTILES, AMPHIBIANS, AND INVERTEBRATES

PLANTS

Reptiles
(Federal and State)

Atlantic Hawksbill Sea Turtle

Kemp's Ridley Sea Turtle

Leatherback Sea Turtle

Amphibians
(Federal and State)

Barton Springs Salamander

Houston Toad

Texas Blind Salamander

Invertebrates
(Federal and State)

Peck's Cave Amphipod

Ouachita Rock-Pocketbook Mussel

(Federal Only)

Comal Springs Riffle Beetle

• Major City

— Major River

— Major Stream

Plants
(Federal and State)

Little Aguja Pondweed

Texas Snowbell

Texas Wild-Rice

0   50   100   150
Miles

0   50 100 150
Kilometers

Source: Texas Parks and Wildlife Department, 2004.

Invasive Plant Species

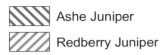

Ashe Juniper

Redberry Juniper

Ashe juniper (*Juniperus ashei*) and redberry juniper (*Juniperus pinchotii*), sometimes called "cedars" in Texas, are a major management concern on rangelands. These trees can reduce plant species production and diversity, restrict accessibility to desired foraging plants, encroach upon grazing areas, and consume large amounts of water. Chinese tallow (*Sapium sebiferum*) was introduced as an agricultural crop from Asia to the Gulf Coast area about 1900. Chinese tallow invaded and eventually dominated a variety of habitats and reduced native plant diversity. Government agencies introduced salt cedar (*Tamarix hispida rubra*) from Eurasia to the western United States in the 1930s in an effort to reduce erosion. Since then, salt cedar has spread throughout the Southwest. The salt cedar secretes salt from its leaves that accumulates in the soil and water and inhibits the growth of other plants. One tree alone can consume up to 200 gallons of water per day. The U.S. Department of Agriculture provides county-prioritized funding for management practices to control and reduce the Chinese tallow and salt cedar invasions.

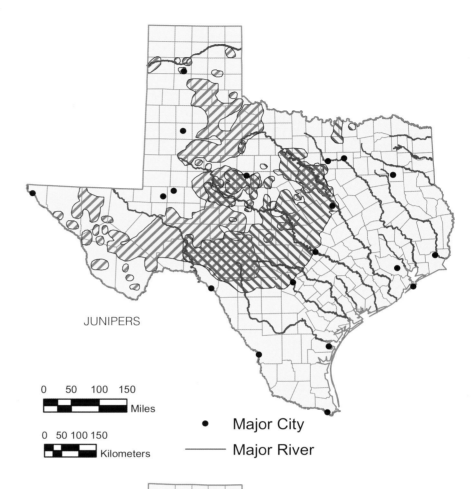

JUNIPERS

0   50   100   150
███████████ Miles

0 50 100 150
███████████ Kilometers

● Major City

— Major River

Funding Priorities

Chinese Tallow   Salt Cedar

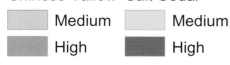

Medium   Medium

High   High

CHINESE TALLOW AND
SALT CEDAR

Sources: Natural Resource Conservation Service, 2004; Texas Agricultural Extension Service, 1998.

Major Protected Areas

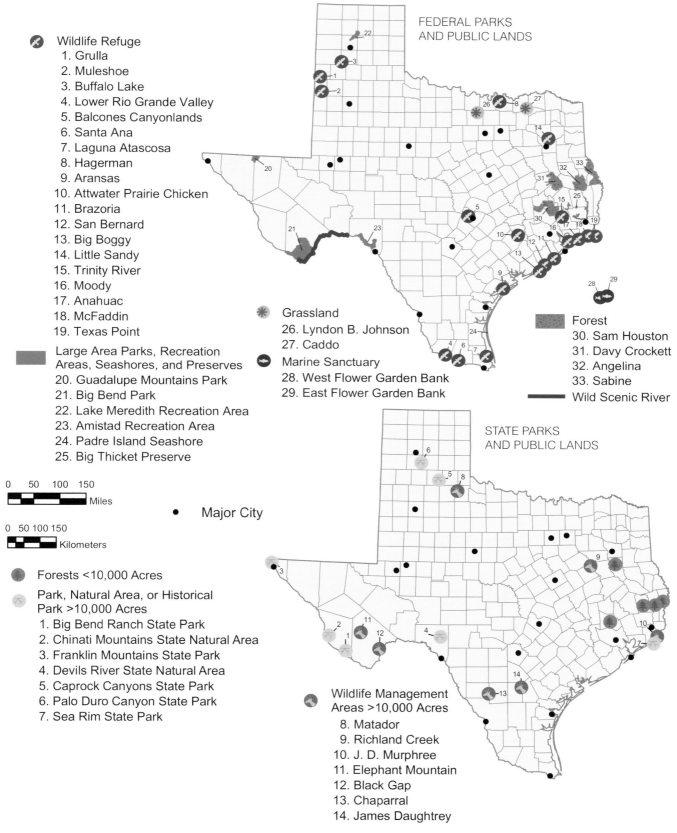

Wildlife Refuge
1. Grulla
2. Muleshoe
3. Buffalo Lake
4. Lower Rio Grande Valley
5. Balcones Canyonlands
6. Santa Ana
7. Laguna Atascosa
8. Hagerman
9. Aransas
10. Attwater Prairie Chicken
11. Brazoria
12. San Bernard
13. Big Boggy
14. Little Sandy
15. Trinity River
16. Moody
17. Anahuac
18. McFaddin
19. Texas Point

Large Area Parks, Recreation Areas, Seashores, and Preserves
20. Guadalupe Mountains Park
21. Big Bend Park
22. Lake Meredith Recreation Area
23. Amistad Recreation Area
24. Padre Island Seashore
25. Big Thicket Preserve

0   50   100   150
Miles

0 50 100 150
Kilometers

Forests <10,000 Acres

Park, Natural Area, or Historical Park >10,000 Acres
1. Big Bend Ranch State Park
2. Chinati Mountains State Natural Area
3. Franklin Mountains State Park
4. Devils River State Natural Area
5. Caprock Canyons State Park
6. Palo Duro Canyon State Park
7. Sea Rim State Park

Grassland
26. Lyndon B. Johnson
27. Caddo

Marine Sanctuary
28. West Flower Garden Bank
29. East Flower Garden Bank

Major City

Forest
30. Sam Houston
31. Davy Crockett
32. Angelina
33. Sabine

Wild Scenic River

FEDERAL PARKS AND PUBLIC LANDS

STATE PARKS AND PUBLIC LANDS

Wildlife Management Areas >10,000 Acres
8. Matador
9. Richland Creek
10. J. D. Murphree
11. Elephant Mountain
12. Black Gap
13. Chaparral
14. James Daughtrey

Sources: National Park Service, 2000; U.S. Fish and Wildlife Service, 2002; U.S. Forest Service, 2002; Texas Natural Resources Information System, 2002; National Oceanic and Atmospheric Administration, 2002.

6 Water Recreation

HAVING 1.26 MILLION SURFACE ACRES OF freshwater in lakes, 2.1 million surface acres in saltwater bays, and more than 80,000 miles of rivers and streams, Texas has one of the greatest varieties of water bodies of any state in the country. East Texas rivers and bayous flow slowly toward the Gulf of Mexico to provide tranquil recreational experiences through lush vegetation. Central Texas rivers and streams cut through the Hill Country, offering relaxing floats on spring-fed streams and stretches of whitewater for the more adventurous. West Texas rivers and arroyos have formed high bluffs and enormous canyons through arid high plains that paint stark yet stunning landscapes (TPWD 2006).

Texans and visitors from throughout the country and around the world spend billions of dollars on Texas water-related outdoor recreation, particularly swimming, fishing, boating, and tubing. Other outdoor activities, including hunting, bird-watching, and nature studies, are also dependent on water and wetlands (TPWD 2006). In 2001, the overall economic impact of 2.4 million Texas anglers was $4.6 billion, which ranked Texas third in the nation behind Florida and California (American Sportfishing Association 2002).

Cool spring-fed rivers and ponds afford relief from long, hot Texas summers. The warm waters of the Gulf of Mexico offer year-round recreational opportunities for boating, surfing, swimming, and fishing. More than six hundred thousand registered motorboats and personal watercraft ply Texas waterways along with over a million kayakers, canoeists, rafting enthusiasts, sailboarders, and sailors. Pleasure cruisers and anglers crowd marinas and boat ramps, especially in the spring and summer months (TPWD 2006; Webb et al. 2006).

Recreational uses of water resources have thus spawned a large water recreation industry. In a typical year, for example, about five hundred thousand people spend more than $20 million having fun tubing the San Marcos River (Greater San Marcos Economic Development Council 2000). Avid fishers purchase boats and gear costing $30,000 or more to catch a handful of fresh fish a few weekends a year.

Texas aquariums and water and scuba parks are world famous: for example, the Texas State Aquarium in Corpus Christi exhibits hundreds of marine animals; Sea World in San Antonio draws enthusiastic crowds to its fascinating performances; Schlitterbahn (slippery road) Waterpark in New Braunfels attracts thousands each summer to exhilarating water slides and rides; and underwater coral formations off the Gulf of Mexico shoreline form a colorful paradise for scuba divers (AmericanZoos.com 2006; About.com 2006; Texas Diver 2006). Texas waterscapes and water parks provide recreational opportunities to millions of visitors, and the numbers of these water enthusiasts are increasing substantially each year (TPWD 2006).

Water Access by Boats, 2005

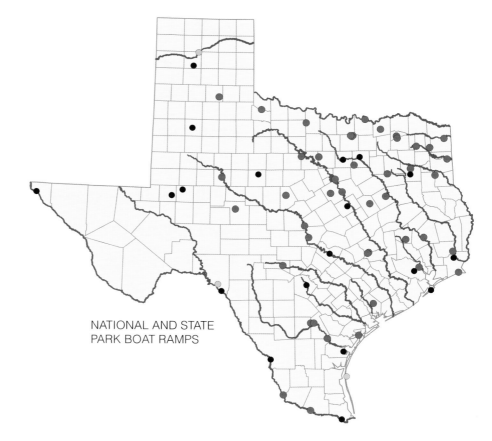

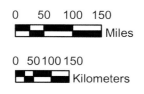

Major City

Major River

Boat Ramp

National Park

State Park

0 50 100 150 Miles

0 50 100 150 Kilometers

NATIONAL AND STATE
PARK BOAT RAMPS

COASTAL AREA FACILITIES

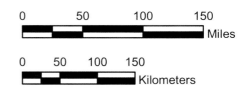

Major City

Major River

Boat Ramp

Marina

Anchorage

0   50   100   150 Miles

0   50   100   150 Kilometers

Sources: Texas Parks and Wildlife Department, 2005; National Park Service, 2005.

Aquariums, 2006

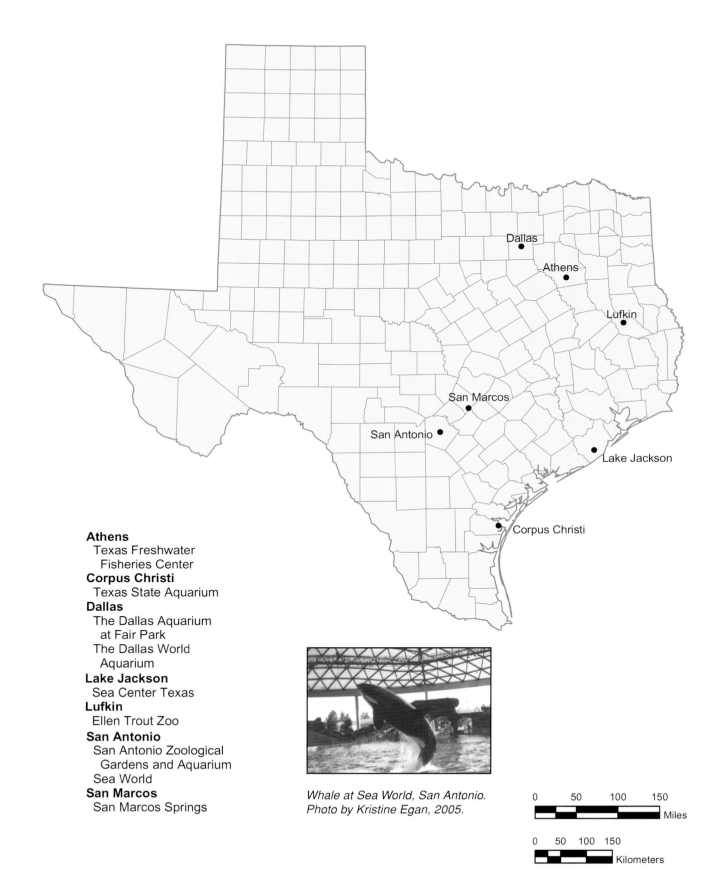

Dallas •
Athens •
Lufkin •
San Marcos •
San Antonio •
Lake Jackson •
Corpus Christi •

Athens
  Texas Freshwater
  Fisheries Center
Corpus Christi
  Texas State Aquarium
Dallas
  The Dallas Aquarium
  at Fair Park
  The Dallas World
  Aquarium
Lake Jackson
  Sea Center Texas
Lufkin
  Ellen Trout Zoo
San Antonio
  San Antonio Zoological
  Gardens and Aquarium
  Sea World
San Marcos
  San Marcos Springs

Whale at Sea World, San Antonio.
Photo by Kristine Egan, 2005.

0   50   100   150
Miles

0   50   100   150
Kilometers

Source: Zoos & Aquariums, 2006.

Water Parks, 2006

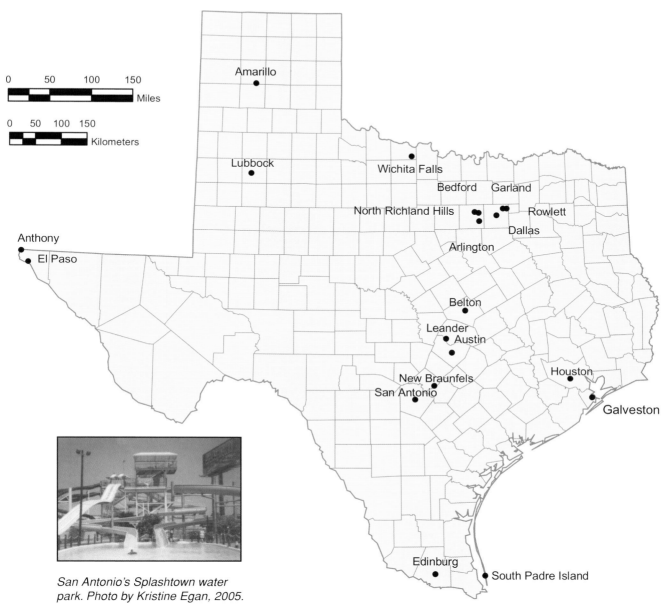

Map labels:
Amarillo
Lubbock
Wichita Falls
Bedford · Garland
North Richland Hills · Rowlett
Dallas
Anthony
El Paso
Arlington
Belton
Leander
Austin
New Braunfels
Houston
San Antonio
Galveston
Edinburg
South Padre Island

Scale:
0 50 100 150 Miles
0 50 100 150 Kilometers

San Antonio's Splashtown water park. Photo by Kristine Egan, 2005.

Water Parks

Anthony
Wet 'n' Wild Water World
Arlington
Hurricane Harbor
Bedford
Bedford Splash
Belton
Summer Fun USA
Edinburg
SuperSplash
Galveston
Schlitterbahn Galveston

Garland
Hawaiian Falls
Houston
Adventure Bay
Splashtown
Waterworld
Leander
Volente Beach
Lubbock
Texas Water Rampage
New Braunfels
Schlitterbahn

North Richland Hills
NR H$_2$O
Rowlett
The Wet Zone
San Antonio
Armadillo Beach
Lost Lagoon
Splashtown
South Padre Island
Schlitterbahn Beach
Wichita Falls
Castaway Cove

Theme Parks with Water Parks

Amarillo
Wonderland Park
Arlington
Six Flags over Texas
Dallas
Sandy Lake
El Paso
Western Playland
Houston
Astroworld
Lubbock
Joyland

San Antonio
Fiesta Texas
Sea World

Source: About, 2006.

Scuba Parks, 2006

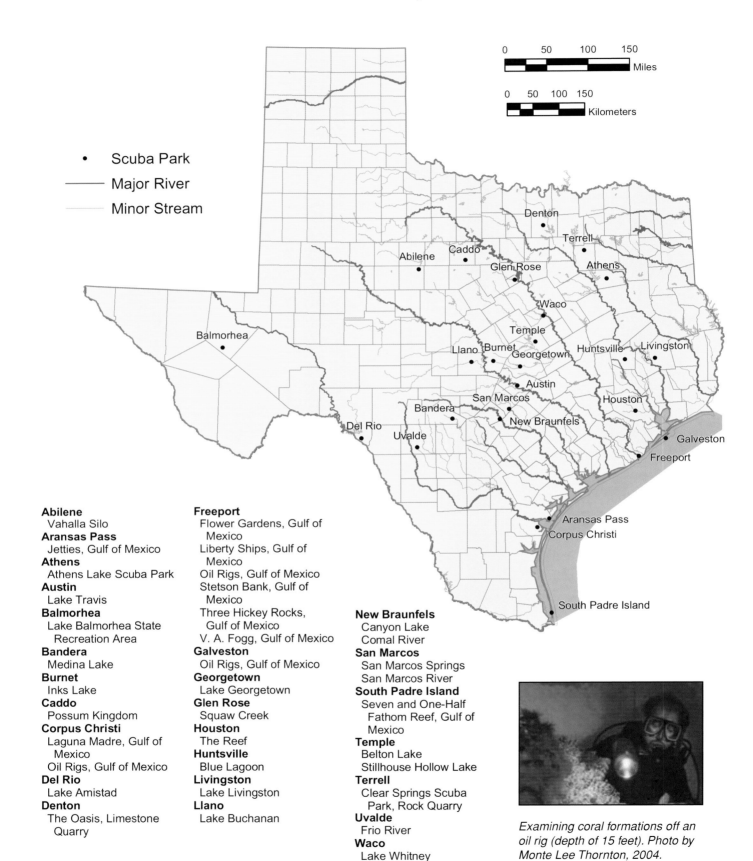

Abilene
  Vahalla Silo
Aransas Pass
  Jetties, Gulf of Mexico
Athens
  Athens Lake Scuba Park
Austin
  Lake Travis
Balmorhea
  Lake Balmorhea State
  Recreation Area
Bandera
  Medina Lake
Burnet
  Inks Lake
Caddo
  Possum Kingdom
Corpus Christi
  Laguna Madre, Gulf of
  Mexico
  Oil Rigs, Gulf of Mexico
Del Rio
  Lake Amistad
Denton
  The Oasis, Limestone
  Quarry

Freeport
  Flower Gardens, Gulf of
  Mexico
  Liberty Ships, Gulf of
  Mexico
  Oil Rigs, Gulf of Mexico
  Stetson Bank, Gulf of
  Mexico
  Three Hickey Rocks,
  Gulf of Mexico
  V. A. Fogg, Gulf of Mexico
Galveston
  Oil Rigs, Gulf of Mexico
Georgetown
  Lake Georgetown
Glen Rose
  Squaw Creek
Houston
  The Reef
Huntsville
  Blue Lagoon
Livingston
  Lake Livingston
Llano
  Lake Buchanan

New Braunfels
  Canyon Lake
  Comal River
San Marcos
  San Marcos Springs
  San Marcos River
South Padre Island
  Seven and One-Half
  Fathom Reef, Gulf of
  Mexico
Temple
  Belton Lake
  Stillhouse Hollow Lake
Terrell
  Clear Springs Scuba
  Park, Rock Quarry
Uvalde
  Frio River
Waco
  Lake Whitney

Examining coral formations off an oil rig (depth of 15 feet). Photo by Monte Lee Thornton, 2004.

Source: Texas Diver, 2006; Dive Texas, 2006.

Tubing Access, 2006

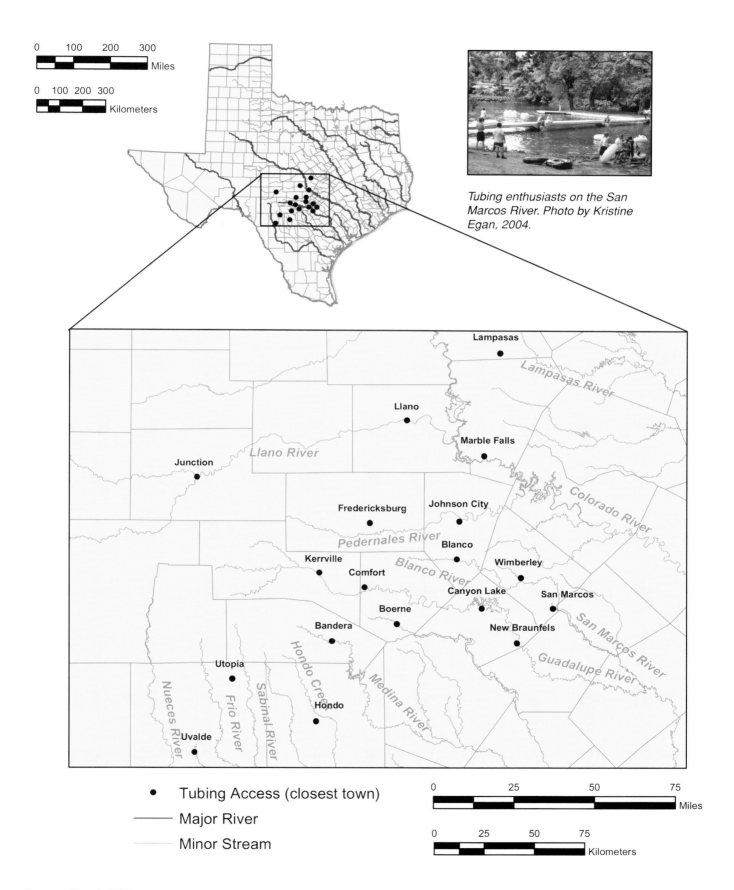

0   100   200   300
Miles

0   100 200 300
Kilometers

Tubing enthusiasts on the San Marcos River. Photo by Kristine Egan, 2004.

Lampasas

Lampasas River

Llano

Marble Falls

Junction

Llano River

Fredericksburg   Johnson City

Pedernales River   Blanco

Colorado River

Kerrville   Comfort   Blanco River   Wimberley

Canyon Lake   San Marcos

Boerne   New Braunfels

San Marcos River

Bandera   Guadalupe River

Hondo Creek   Medina River

Utopia

Nueces River   Frio River   Sabinal River   Hondo

Uvalde

● Tubing Access (closest town)

— Major River

— Minor Stream

0   25   50   75
Miles

0   25   50   75
Kilometers

Source: About, 2006.

7 Water Prospects

W HAT DOES THE FUTURE HOLD FOR water resources in Texas? The population of Texas is expected to expand dramatically from 20.9 million in 2000 to 33.3 million in 2030 and to 45.6 million in 2060 (U.S. Census Bureau 2005; TWDB 2007). Concomitantly, water demand is expected to increase from the current 17 million acre-feet annually to 22 million acre-feet in 2060 (TPWD 2007). Because of the already stretched use of water supplies, a shift will occur away from wasteful uses of water toward those that are more profitable to society. The increased competition for the state's finite water supply will result in increased government-mandated management and restrictions. Greater competition for the state's water will force the use of water supplies that traditionally have been too expensive, such as desalinated water, and will drive a stronger statewide philosophy regarding conservation and reuse of existing water supplies (TWDB 2002–2006; SAWS 2004–2006).

In projections of major inventory categories of water usage, municipal, steam and electric, and manufacturing will more than double by 2060 and increase far more substantially than the decrease of water usage in irrigation, livestock, and mining (TWDB 2005). Water for recreation will become more important as its economic impact grows. An increasingly urban and affluent population will spend sizable amounts of money on the pleasures of water recreation.

As shown in this atlas, droughts and overuse of the state's water supply have led to increased regulation of its use, thereby restricting landowners' freedom to utilize water as they desire. The mid-1990s "mini-drought" caused major agricultural losses and provoked the passage of Senate Bill 1 in 1997. This legislation mandated the creation of water management regions and the development of drought management plans by public water suppliers that have more than one hundred customers, both public and private (Texas Water Law Institute 1997). Pro-viding sufficient freshwater inflows to the bays and estuaries is now a legal mandate that must be considered in the process of approving water permits. Even the rule of capture in groundwater law, sacrosanct since the 1904 *Houston RR v. East* decision, is being interpreted in an ever-narrower way. As specified in the 2001 Senate Bill 2, for instance, groundwater conservation districts can now limit the amount the water that "nonhistoric" users withdraw.

The increase in demand and the overexploitation of readily available, inexpensive water supplies have resulted in the utilization of water resources that were rejected as recently as the 1980s. Local supplies that cost less than $200 per acre-foot are no longer available. More expensive alternatives, such as interbasin transfers and desalination, have gained currency even though their delivered costs are often greater than $1,000 per acre-foot. Because of the high costs of additional supplies, there has been a new impetus for water conservation and reuse of water. Most implemented water conservation programs, such as low-flow plumbing fixtures and xeriscaping, produce water savings of less than $1,000 per acre-foot. Municipal wastewater can be cleansed for less than $1,000 per acre-foot, which has already enabled its widespread use for landscaping and industrial uses (HDR Engineering 2001). The increasing cost of water has led to a shift from less profitable uses to higher-value uses. In many instances, cities have purchased agricultural water rights outright. Elsewhere, cities have paid for increases in agricultural water use efficiency and have recovered the amount conserved.

In conclusion, with the increasing population of Texas and with the state's limited ability to expand its usable water supplies, water and its uses will become more expensive. The use of nontraditional sources of water, such as from desalination, reuse, and interbasin transfers, will enlarge. Government oversight will likewise intensify, especially in periods of drought.

Projected Change in Water Supplies, 2000–2050

Water Management Regions

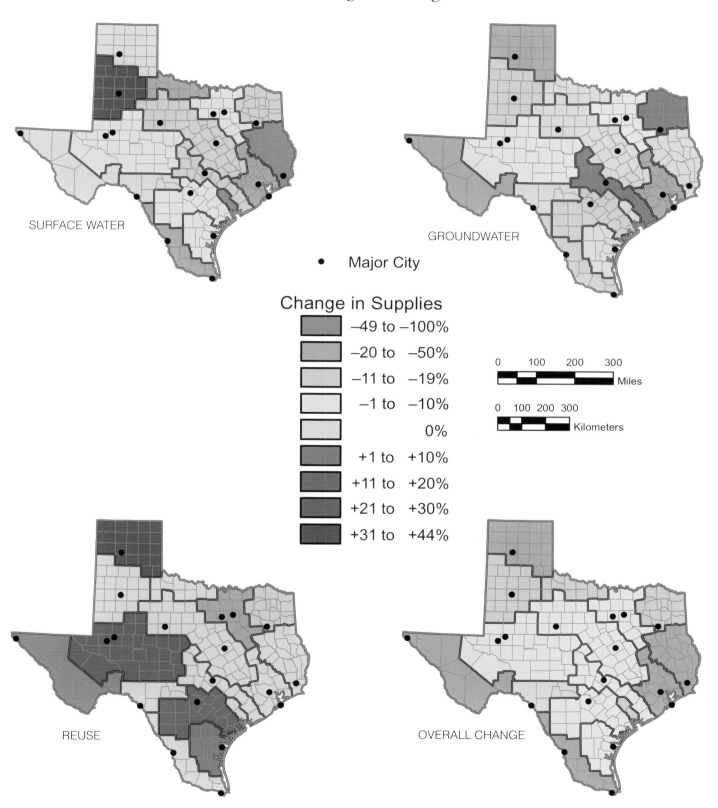

SURFACE WATER

GROUNDWATER

● Major City

Change in Supplies

	−49 to −100%
	−20 to −50%
	−11 to −19%
	−1 to −10%
	0%
	+1 to +10%
	+11 to +20%
	+21 to +30%
	+31 to +44%

0   100   200   300
Miles

0   100   200   300
Kilometers

REUSE

OVERALL CHANGE

Source: Texas Water Development Board, *Water for Texas,* 2002.

Change in Groundwater Supplies, 2000–2050

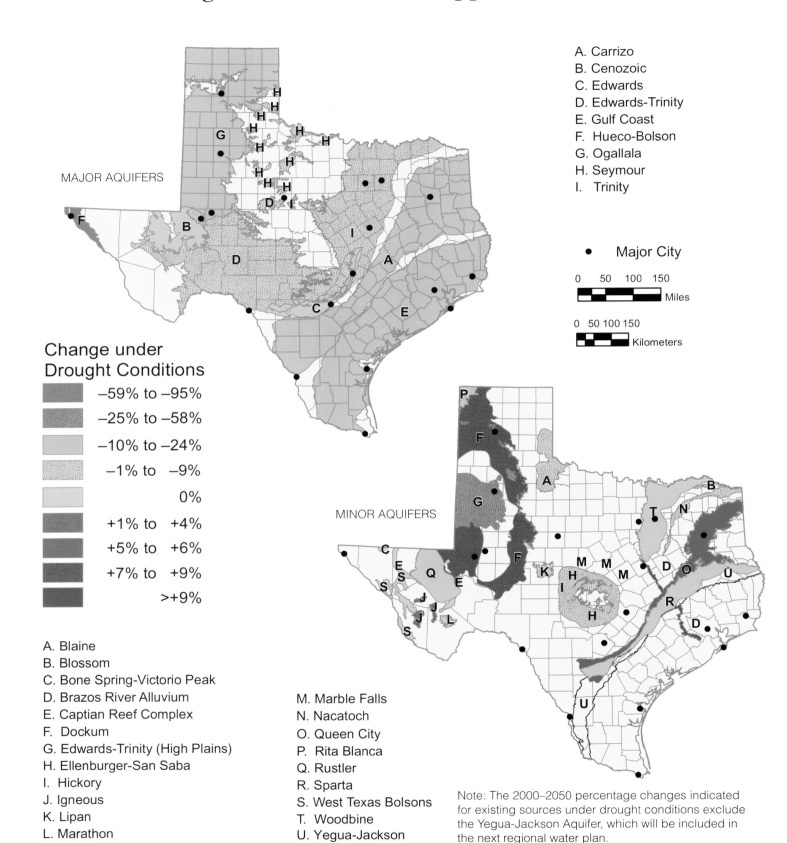

MAJOR AQUIFERS

A. Carrizo
B. Cenozoic
C. Edwards
D. Edwards-Trinity
E. Gulf Coast
F. Hueco-Bolson
G. Ogallala
H. Seymour
I. Trinity

● Major City

0 50 100 150 Miles

0 50 100 150 Kilometers

Change under Drought Conditions

- −59% to −95%
- −25% to −58%
- −10% to −24%
- −1% to −9%
- 0%
- +1% to +4%
- +5% to +6%
- +7% to +9%
- >+9%

MINOR AQUIFERS

A. Blaine
B. Blossom
C. Bone Spring-Victorio Peak
D. Brazos River Alluvium
E. Captian Reef Complex
F. Dockum
G. Edwards-Trinity (High Plains)
H. Ellenburger-San Saba
I. Hickory
J. Igneous
K. Lipan
L. Marathon
M. Marble Falls
N. Nacatoch
O. Queen City
P. Rita Blanca
Q. Rustler
R. Sparta
S. West Texas Bolsons
T. Woodbine
U. Yegua-Jackson

Note: The 2000–2050 percentage changes indicated for existing sources under drought conditions exclude the Yegua-Jackson Aquifer, which will be included in the next regional water plan.

Source: Texas Water Development Board, *Water for Texas,* 2002.

Interbasin Water Transfers

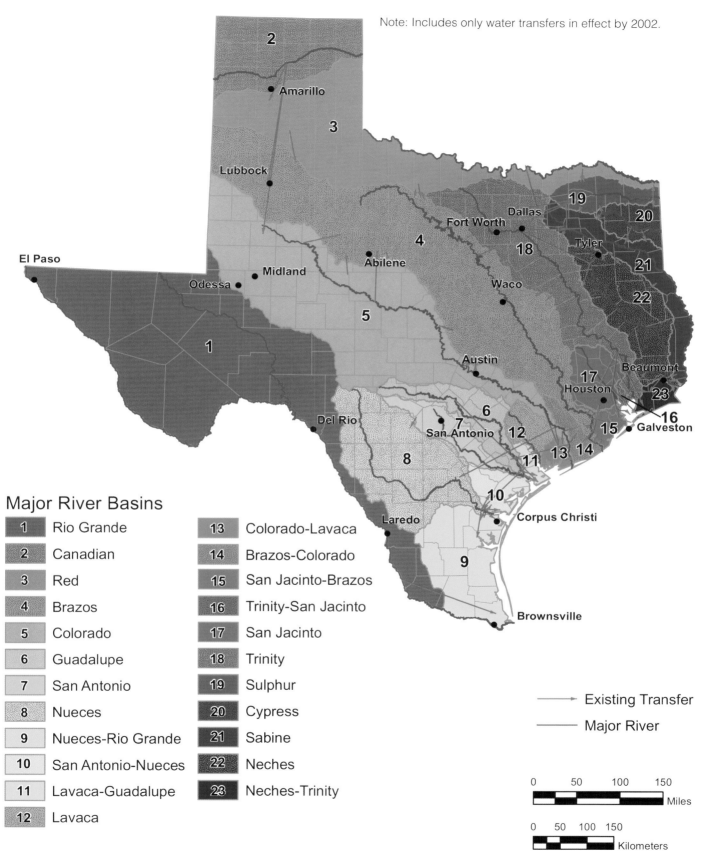

Note: Includes only water transfers in effect by 2002.

Major River Basins

1	Rio Grande	13	Colorado-Lavaca
2	Canadian	14	Brazos-Colorado
3	Red	15	San Jacinto-Brazos
4	Brazos	16	Trinity-San Jacinto
5	Colorado	17	San Jacinto
6	Guadalupe	18	Trinity
7	San Antonio	19	Sulphur
8	Nueces	20	Cypress
9	Nueces-Rio Grande	21	Sabine
10	San Antonio-Nueces	22	Neches
11	Lavaca-Guadalupe	23	Neches-Trinity
12	Lavaca		

→ Existing Transfer
— Major River

0   50   100   150   Miles
0   50 100 150   Kilometers

Source: Texas Water Development Board, *Water for Texas*, 2002.

99

Proposed Interbasin Water Transfers

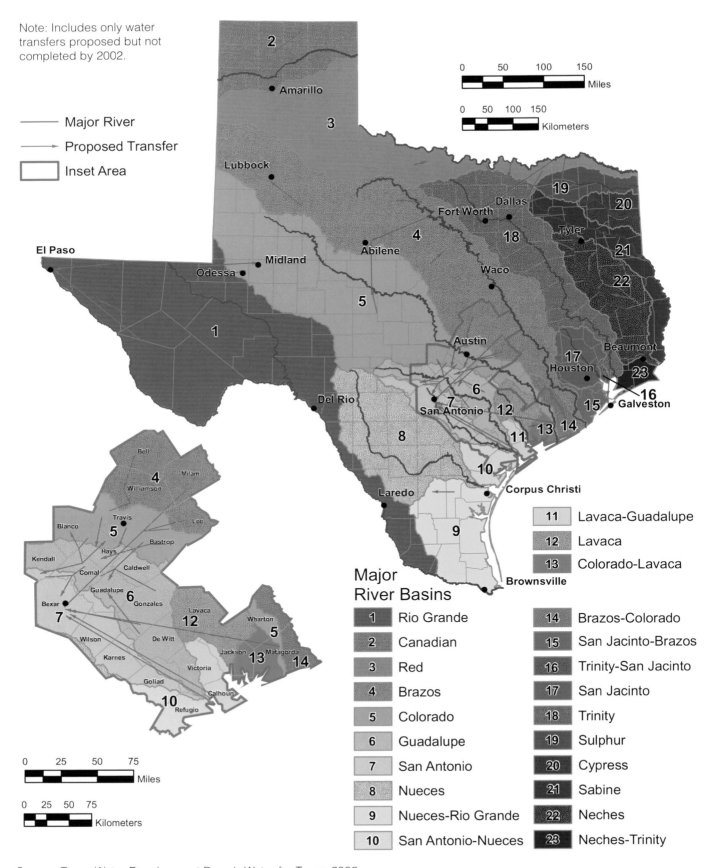

Note: Includes only water transfers proposed but not completed by 2002.

Legend:
— Major River
→ Proposed Transfer
▭ Inset Area

Major River Basins

1 Rio Grande	14 Brazos-Colorado
2 Canadian	15 San Jacinto-Brazos
3 Red	16 Trinity-San Jacinto
4 Brazos	17 San Jacinto
5 Colorado	18 Trinity
6 Guadalupe	19 Sulphur
7 San Antonio	20 Cypress
8 Nueces	21 Sabine
9 Nueces-Rio Grande	22 Neches
10 San Antonio-Nueces	23 Neches-Trinity
11 Lavaca-Guadalupe	
12 Lavaca	
13 Colorado-Lavaca	

Source: Texas Water Development Board, *Water for Texas*, 2002.

Projected Water Needs
Water User Groups in River Basins

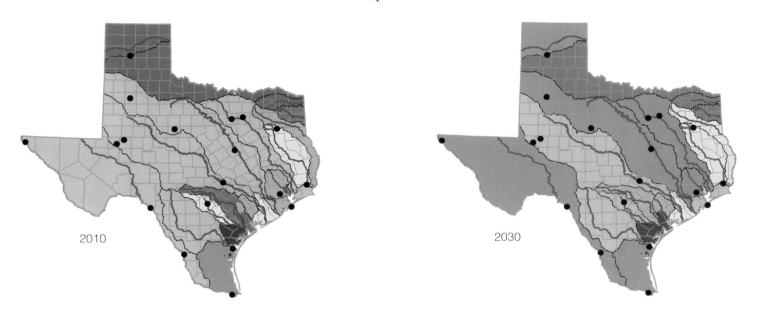

2010

2030

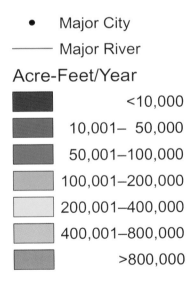

●   Major City

——   Major River

Acre-Feet/Year

▨	<10,000
▨	10,001– 50,000
▨	50,001–100,000
▨	100,001–200,000
▨	200,001–400,000
▨	400,001–800,000
▨	>800,000

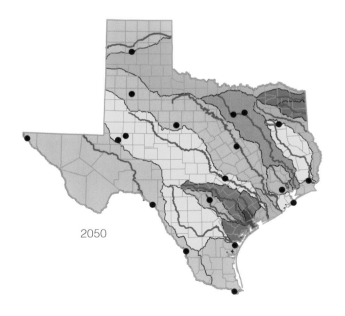

2050

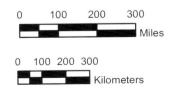

Note: Water user groups are cities with populations of 500 and greater and a county aggregate of demand for other sectors such as irrigation, livestock, manufacturing, mining, and steam-electric power generation.

Source: Texas Water Development Board, *Water for Texas,* 2002.

Counties with Projected Unmet User Group Needs, 2050

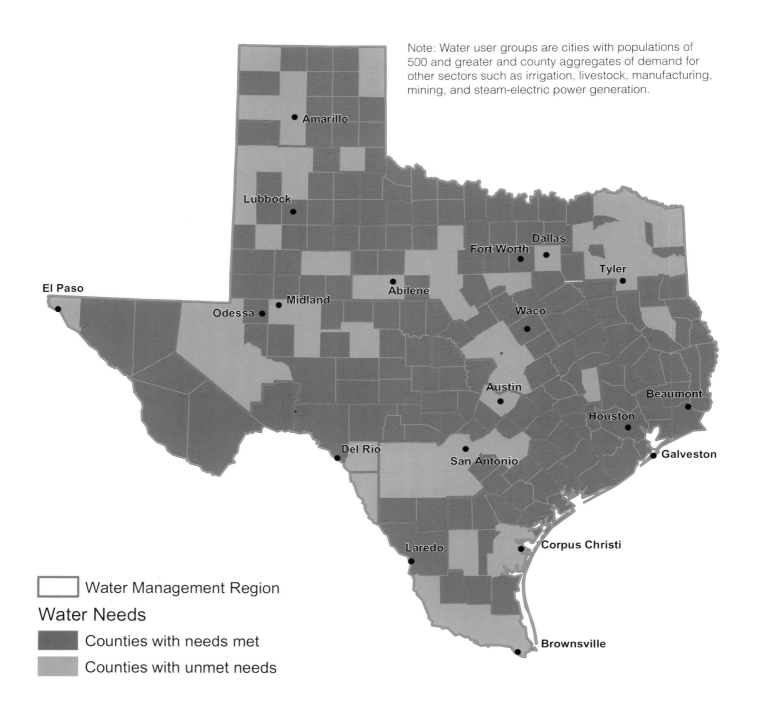

Note: Water user groups are cities with populations of 500 and greater and county aggregates of demand for other sectors such as irrigation, livestock, manufacturing, mining, and steam-electric power generation.

Water Management Region

Water Needs

Counties with needs met

Counties with unmet needs

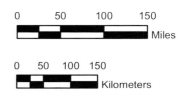

Source: Texas Water Development Board, *Water for Texas*, 2002.

Surface Water Supplies in Drought
Projected for River Basins

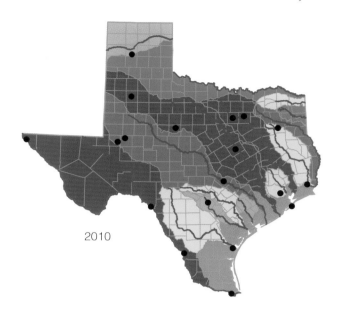

2010

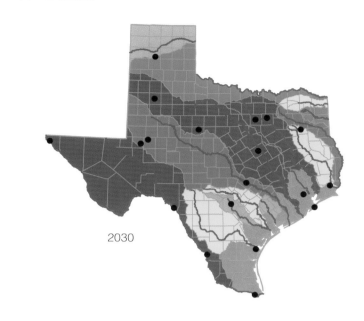

2030

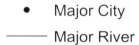
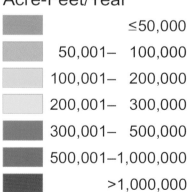

- ●   Major City
- ——   Major River

Acre-Feet/Year

	≤50,000
50,001–	100,000
100,001–	200,000
200,001–	300,000
300,001–	500,000
500,001–1,000,000	
>1,000,000	

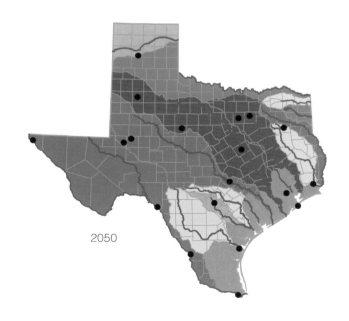

2050

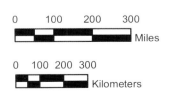

Source: Texas Water Development Board, *Water for Texas*, 2002.

Per Capita Water Use in Drought
Projected for Selected Cities

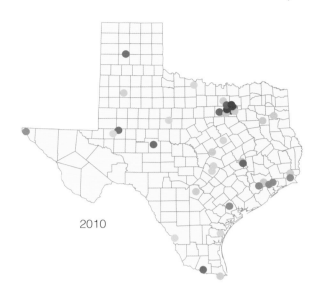

2010

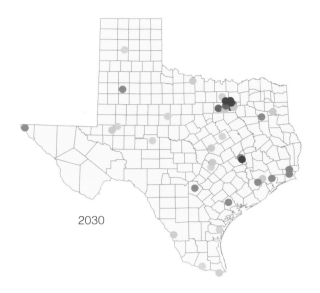

2030

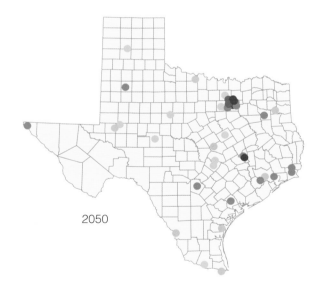

2050

Gallons/Person/Day

- 115–149
- 150–179
- 180–209
- 210–229
- 230–275

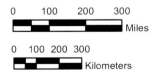

Source: Texas Water Development Board, *Water for Texas*, 2002.

Water Demand Projections
Irrigation

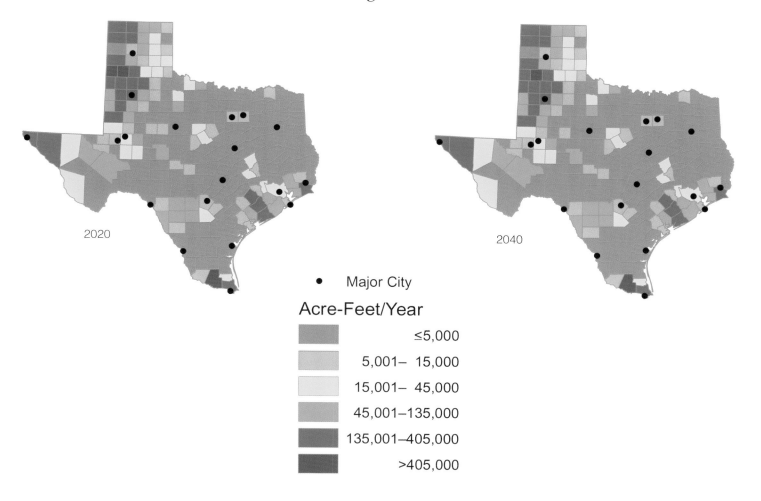

2020

2040

Major City

Acre-Feet/Year

	≤5,000
	5,001– 15,000
	15,001– 45,000
	45,001–135,000
	135,001–405,000
	>405,000

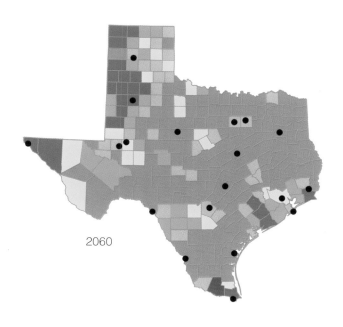

2060

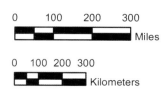

0	100	200	300
Miles

| 0 | 100 | 200 | 300 |
Kilometers

Source: Texas Water Development Board, 2005.

Water Demand Projections
Livestock

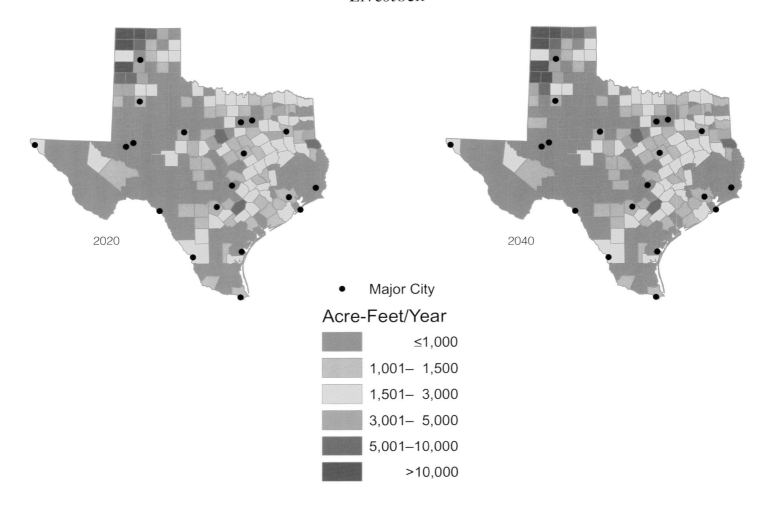

2020

2040

- ● Major City

Acre-Feet/Year

	≤1,000
	1,001– 1,500
	1,501– 3,000
	3,001– 5,000
	5,001–10,000
	>10,000

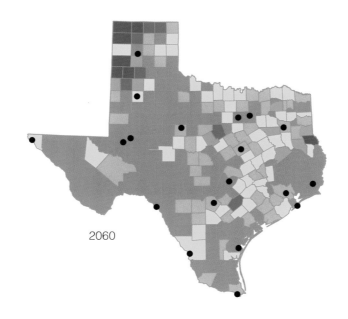

2060

Source: Texas Water Development Board, 2005.

Water Demand Projections
Manufacturing

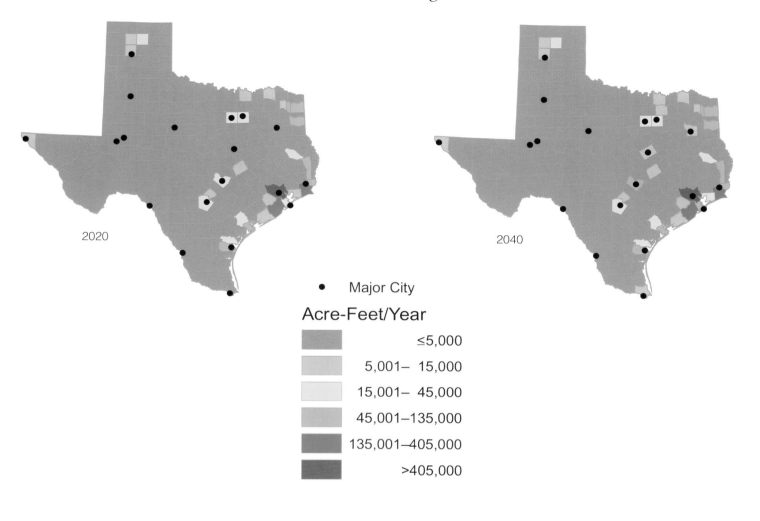

2020

2040

Major City

Acre-Feet/Year

	≤5,000
	5,001– 15,000
	15,001– 45,000
	45,001–135,000
	135,001–405,000
	>405,000

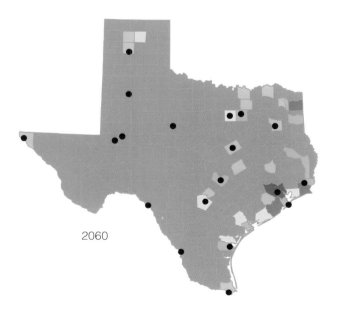

2060

Source: Texas Water Development Board, 2005.

Water Demand Projections
Mining

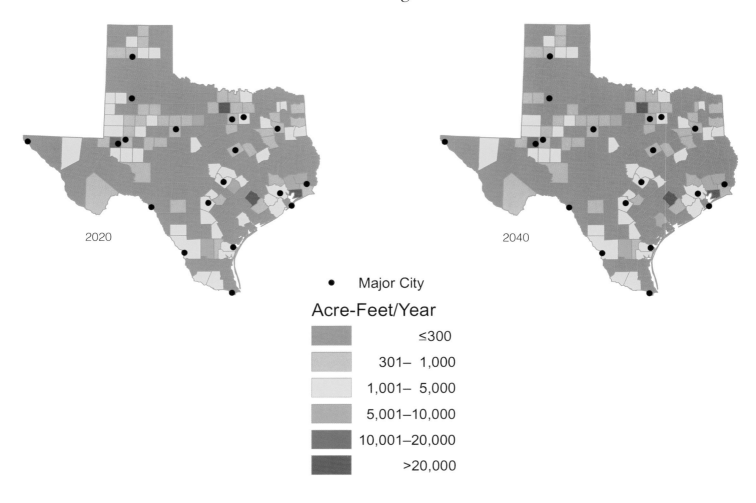

2020

2040

● Major City

Acre-Feet/Year

≤300

301– 1,000

1,001– 5,000

5,001–10,000

10,001–20,000

>20,000

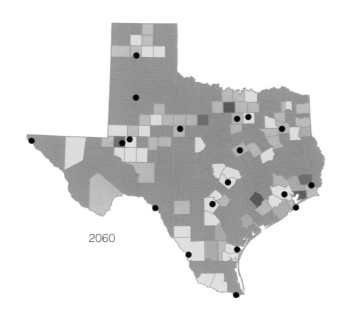

2060

Water Demand Projections
Municipal

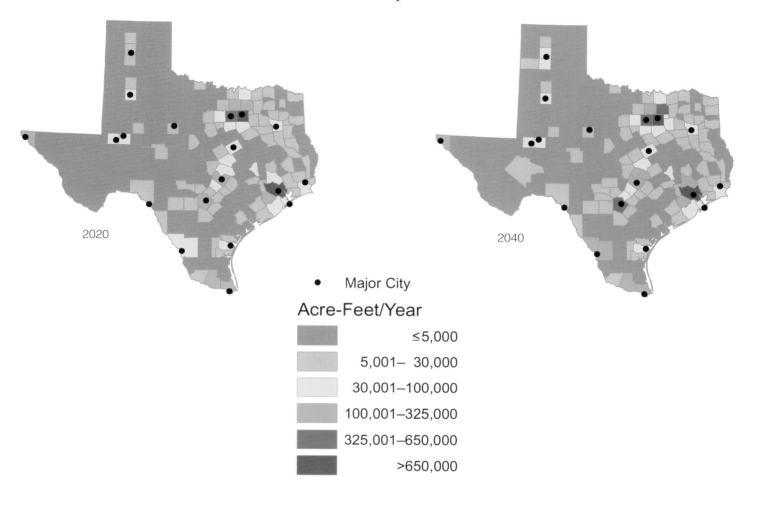

2020

2040

Major City

Acre-Feet/Year

	≤5,000
	5,001– 30,000
	30,001–100,000
	100,001–325,000
	325,001–650,000
	>650,000

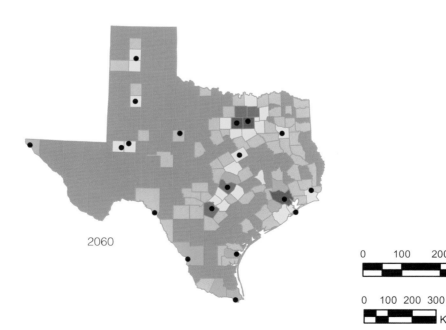

2060

0	100	200	300	
				Miles

0	100	200	300	
				Kilometers

Source: Texas Water Development Board, 2005.

Water Demand Projections
Steam and Electric

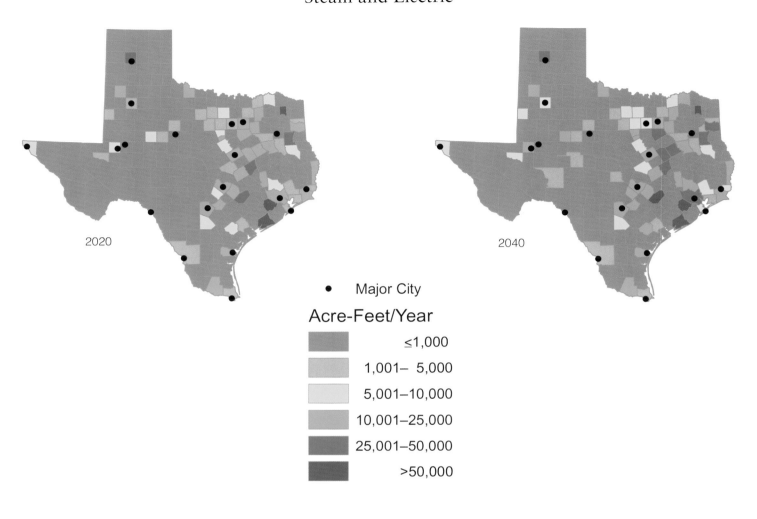

2020

2040

Acre-Feet/Year

● Major City

	≤1,000
	1,001– 5,000
	5,001–10,000
	10,001–25,000
	25,001–50,000
	>50,000

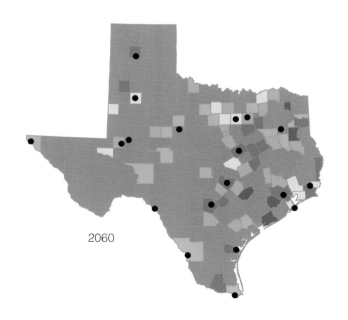

2060

0   100   200   300
Miles

0   100 200 300
Kilometers

Source: Texas Water Development Board, 2006.

Texas Water Timeline

65 million years ago A meteorite crashed into the ocean on the northern edge of Mexico's Yucatán Peninsula. The impact not only resulted in mass extinction to major life-forms of the age but also caused a huge wave that carried debris as far north as the present-day banks of the Brazos River in Falls County.

12,000 years ago At the end of the last glacial episode, the first humans to arrive in present-day Texas settled on the shores of Lubbock Lake. Anthropologists have found other evidence of early humans in Texas at Spring Lake in San Marcos.

3,500 years ago Corn farmers established the oldest continuously cultivated farmland in Texas near the confluence of the Rio Grande and Mexico's Río Concho.

1542 During his expedition to find the Seven Cities of Cíbola, Francisco Vásquez de Coronado noted that the Indians had developed and established irrigation systems near the sites of present-day El Paso and Pecos by diverting water from the Rio Grande and the Pecos River.

1680 Franciscans became the first Europeans to practice irrigation in Texas by beginning the construction of acequias (irrigation ditches) to supply water for domestic use and irrigation near Ysleta on the Rio Grande below El Paso. These first acequias eventually became part of a large irrigation network, portions of which were still in use in the late twentieth century.

1690 Gen. Alonzo de Leon discovered the Trinity River two days before the Feast of the Most Holy Trinity.

1716 Franciscan missionaries began the construction of the most extensive network of acequias in Texas in San Antonio and the surrounding area. Parts of one rock-lined acequia madre (mother ditch) are still in use today.

1718 In their settlement of San Antonio, the Spanish introduced the riparian doctrine that gave landowners water rights to their riparian land.

1805 Spain proclaimed the Red River to be the northern and eastern boundaries of Spanish Texas.

1819 The Adams-Onís Treaty, signed by the United States and Spain, renounced the French claim that Louisiana extended to the Rio Grande and the U.S. claim to Texas. The Red River was again formally established as the northern boundary of Texas.

1821 Attracted by rich soil, good water, and adequate timber, Stephen F. Austin and his group of 300 colonist families settled on the Texas coastal plains between the Colorado and Brazos rivers.

The Red River became the thoroughfare by which many pioneer settlers moved into northern Texas.

1834–35 Capt. Henry Shreve removed the "great raft," a mass of driftwood, trees, and other vegetation that obstructed the upper Red River channel for 75 miles and hampered navigation, thereby allowing a greater flow of traffic west into Texas.

1836 Although Mexico refused to recognize Texas independence, the newly formed Congress of the Republic of Texas proclaimed that the Rio Grande, from its mouth to its source, formed the republic's western and southern boundaries with Mexico.

Numerous packet boats steamed up the Trinity River with cargo consisting of groceries and dry goods in exchange for cotton, sugar, cowhides, and deerskins.

1837 In October, "Racer's Storm," a strong wind named for the British sloop-of-war that encountered the phenomenon in the Yucatán channel, wrecked nearly every vessel on the Texas coast and blew away all the houses on Galveston Island. The tropical storm flooded the coastal prairies 15 to 20 miles inland.

The Congress of the Republic of Texas established the General Land Office (GLO) to administer and manage the public land of Texas.

1840 The Texas Congress adopted the English common law riparian principle that gave riparian landowners the right to reasonable use of water for irrigation or for other purposes.

1842 Major flooding occurred on the Brazos River from Washington to Navasota, widening the river to 6 miles or more for an extended distance.

The side-wheeler *Mustang* became the first steamboat to unload cargo at Washington on the Brazos River.

A hurricane struck Galveston in September, causing heavy damage in some areas, but no lives were lost.

1845   The U.S. Congress approved the Texas state constitution, and on December 29 Pres. James K. Polk signed the act admitting Texas as a state.

1848   With the Treaty of Guadalupe Hidalgo, which terminated the Mexican War, the Rio Grande became the international boundary between the United States and Mexico.

1849   The U.S. Congress recognized the Texas claim that its eastern boundary with Louisiana ran through the middle of Sabine Lake.

1854   The introduction of the windmill, used primarily for pumping water for farming and household needs, was crucial to the survival of farmers in Texas' semiarid High Plains region.

A canal between the Port of Galveston and the Brazos River opened.

In September, a hurricane struck Texas between Matagorda and Galveston, leveling the Matagorda community.

1856   Over the years, a logjam formed in the Red River for 30 miles above Shreveport and backed up the waters of Big Cypress Creek to form Caddo Lake.

1857   On the plains of West Texas, John Pope began experimenting with drilling for artesian wells.

1858   The Texas legislature authorized artesian well drilling between San Antonio and Laredo.

1866   A privately owned water-distribution system from wells began in San Antonio.

1867   In a report to the War Department, Lt. Col. S. D. Sturgis wrote that the water of the Brazos River was so briny that not even mules would drink it.

In October, a hurricane flattened Bagdad and Clarksville at the mouth of the Rio Grande and flooded Galveston.

1868   Large-scale irrigation began in Texas with the construction of canals near Del Rio.

After a voyage of a year and four days, steamboat *Job Boat No. 1* traveled up the Trinity River from Galveston to deposit cargo in Dallas.

1869   The largest flood on record swept through the Colorado River Valley and caused major damage from Austin to the Gulf Coast.

1870   The Waco Suspension Bridge became the first bridge across the Brazos River.

1870s Construction of large-scale irrigation canals began on the Pecos River, in the lower Rio Grande Valley, and in the Fort Stockton area.

The Rio Grande cut deep into its banks on the Mexico side, gradually transferring land to the United States and causing the international Chamizal dispute in El Paso.

1872   The Texas Supreme Court noted the unsuitability of the state's riparian regulations in arid and semi-arid regions and suggested corrective action.

1874   The logjam that had hindered navigation on the upper Red River for almost 25 years was removed.

1875   In September, a hurricane killed 176 people and washed away 75 percent of the buildings in Indianola, Calhoun County.

1880   A tropical storm in October killed many people and nearly destroyed Brownsville.

1881   Dallas began construction of a sanitary sewer.

1884   The United States and Mexico signed a boundary treaty that addressed changes of the Rio Grande channel. In the agreement, gradual erosion or accretion changes allowed for boundary changes through new channels. Sudden river course changes, however, would not create new boundaries.

1886   A hurricane struck the town of Indianola in August, destroying or damaging every structure.

1889   A boundary agreement between the United States and Mexico established a commission to process all disputes caused by changes in the Rio Grande.

An irrigation act addressed the development of the arid West Texas agricultural irrigation systems and declared nonappropriated river and natural stream water to be state property.

1890   Austin voters approved $1.4 million in bonds to construct a dam to provide a reliable source of water and electricity.

1890s Construction of large-scale irrigation canals began in the El Paso area and in the Coastal Plain.

1893   The Austin granite-and-limestone dam was completed.

1894   Workers drilling for water in Corsicana discovered oil.

1895   An irrigation act extended state waters subject to appropriation to include the ordinary, underground, and storm water flows of natural rivers.

The act did not revoke preexisting riparian water rights.

1897   The Blackland and Grand Prairie regions had 458 flowing and 506 nonflowing artesian wells. Few artesian wells were located on the Coastal Plain, and the High Plains had none.

1899   On June 17–28, rainfall over 66,000 square miles averaged 8.9 inches and caused major flooding of the Brazos River. Property damage exceeded $9 million, 284 people died, and thousands of others lost their homes.

1900   In September, the "Great Hurricane," the worst natural disaster in U.S. history, destroyed much of Galveston. Flooding caused most of the damage. Property loss totaled about $40 million, and an estimated 6,000 to 8,000 people died.

Heavy rains falling on the Colorado River watershed caused the river to crest 11 feet above the Austin Dam, ultimately destroying it.

1902   Towns and counties along the river established the Brazos River Impoundment Association to try to manage the river and its watershed.

1904   *Houston RR v. East* confirmed the English law of the rule of capture. This law allows landowners to pump as much groundwater as can be put to beneficial use, regardless of the impact on neighboring wells. The Texas Supreme Court has upheld the law several times (most recently in 1999).

A constitutional amendment authorized the first public development of water resources.

1905   The Texas legislature approved the formation of the first drainage districts.

The federal Rivers and Harbors Act provided funds for the construction of a lock-and-dam system on the Brazos River between Waco and Washington.

Defining the exact international border along the Rio Grande in relationship to bancos (wide oxbows that overflow and form new channels) was resolved through the Banco Treaty.

In the "Artesian Belt," most of South Texas from Corpus Christi to the Rio Grande Valley, 200 wells were in operation. Wells ranged in depth from 600 to 800 feet and had average flows from 200 to 600 gallons per minute.

1908   The Trinity River's most disastrous flood on record occurred.

1911   The Houston Street viaduct in Dallas was completed.

1912   The Medina River Dam was completed for irrigation.

1913   An irrigation act established the Texas Board of Water Engineers to create procedures for determining surface water rights. The board declared all nonappropriated waters in the state to be the property of the state and abolished riparian rights that applied to lands acquired from the state after 1895.

The state Water Code confirmed the rule of capture. The code defined groundwater as "percolating waters" that are distinct from subterranean streams with well-defined flows and channels. Exceptions to the rule of capture included deliberate acts of wasting artesian flow, contaminating groundwater, wasting water to injure another, causing subsidence due to negligent overpumping, and slanting wells to remove water from someone else's property.

Both the Guadalupe and Trinity rivers flooded.

The Brazos and Colorado rivers flooded more than 3,000 square miles of land, causing the deaths of 177 people and almost $3.5 million in property damage in the Brazos River Valley alone. The huge flood changed the course of the Brazos River to enter the Gulf of Mexico at Freeport and destroyed all the work completed on the river's lock-and-dam system.

1914   The Texas Board of Water Engineers produced its first set of rules and regulations.

The Paddock Viaduct in Fort Worth was completed.

1915   A flood destroyed the rebuilt Austin Dam.

In August, a hurricane battered Galveston, causing $50 million in property damage. A new seawall provided protection, yet 275 lives were lost.

1916   The first activated sludge wastewater treatment plant in the United States was built on the San Marcos River in San Marcos.

A storm struck Corpus Christi in August, causing more than $1.5 million in property damage and taking 20 lives.

1917   A series of dry seasons (1916–18) stimulated renewed interest in constructing storage reservoirs for irrigation.

A constitutional amendment provided for landowner formation of water-conservation and reclamation districts.

In the provisions of the Conservation Amendment to the Texas Constitution, the control, prevention, and distribution of flood and storm waters became the responsibility of the state, and all limitations that had prevented local financing of flood-control projects were removed.

1919   The Texas legislature authorized the formation of freshwater supply districts.

A hurricane struck just south of Corpus Christi in September, caused more than $20 million in property damage, and killed 284 people.

1920   Development of large-scale irrigation canals began on the High Plains.

1921   The Brazos River experienced major flooding that brought death and destruction of a greater magnitude than had previously been experienced.

A record flood in September extensively damaged the San Antonio business district.

1923   Water power in Texas produced energy for ginning cotton, grinding corn, sawing lumber, and generating electricity.

The Texas legislature approved funding for a survey of all rivers and an analysis of flood and water problems.

1925   The Texas legislature authorized the formation of water control and improvement districts.

Dredging of the Houston Ship Channel made possible the Port of Houston, located 50 miles from the deep water in the Gulf of Mexico.

1926   The Texas Supreme Court, in the landmark case *Motl v. Boyd*, upheld that Spanish and pre-1840 republic land grants carried extensive riparian rights, including the right to irrigate with water from associated streams.

The Olmos Reservoir in the San Antonio River Basin was completed to provide flood protection to the city's downtown district 4 miles south.

1929   The Texas legislature created the first river authority, Brazos River Authority (BRA), with the mission to conserve, control, and utilize the storm and floodwaters of the river and its tributary streams.

Flooding removed a logjam that had limited navigation on the Colorado River.

1931   A Texas subsidiary of a Chicago-based utility company began building the Hamilton Dam on the Colorado River in Burnet County.

The Texas legislature passed a law designed to prevent artesian water wastage.

The Wagstaff Act, which was never applied, gave domestic and municipal water users priority during designated drought periods.

1932   The United States and Mexico agreed on the Lower Rio Grande Valley Flood Control Project, which was to strengthen and raise levees and dredge the channel and floodways.

1933   The dust bowl drought began on the High Plains and lasted 44 months, until August 1936.

The Texas legislature authorized the formation of water supply districts.

The United States and Mexico approved the Rio Grande Rectification Treaty, which straightened the river's channel east of El Paso. The treaty also provided for construction of toll-free bridges between three pairs of U.S.-Mexican towns on the Rio Grande.

In September, a hurricane hit near Brownsville and killed 40 people, injured 500, and destroyed most of the citrus crop of the lower Rio Grande Valley.

1934   Pres. Franklin D. Roosevelt announced that the Public Works Administration would assist in the completion of Buchanan Dam.

Caused by poor land management practices and sustained drought conditions (three waves: 1934, 1936, and 1939–40), great dust storms spread throughout the Great Plains. The drought, which lasted as long as eight years in some areas and severely affected 27 states, was the worst in U.S. history.

1935   Pres. Franklin D. Roosevelt approved the Emergency Relief Appropriations Act, which provided $525 million for drought relief.

The Texas legislature created the Guadalupe-Blanco River Authority (GBRA) for the lower Guadalupe River watershed.

The Texas legislature created the Lower Colorado River Authority (LCRA) for the 600-mile reach of the Texas Colorado River between San Saba and the Gulf Coast.

The Texas legislature created the Sabine-Neches River Conservation District; however, this organization was inactive until 1949.

The Texas legislature created the Nueces River Authority (NRA), which served all or part of 22 counties in South Texas.

The U.S. Congress established the Soil Conservation Service in the Department of Agriculture. The new agency helped establish the precedent of paying farmers to practice soil-conserving farming techniques.

The BRA completed its first master plan for reservoir development, including 13 dams on the Brazos River and its tributaries.

| 1936 | About 600 wells irrigated 80,000 acres in the High Plains, El Paso Valley, Winter Garden District, and Gulf Coast Plains. |

The U.S. Congress passed the Flood Control Act, which authorized the construction of flood-control facilities by the U.S. Soil Conservation Service and the U.S. Army Corps of Engineers (USACE). The Corps of Engineers constructed many flood-control dams on Texas rivers, and the Soil Conservation Service did so on tributary watersheds.

1937   The LCRA completed the construction of Hamilton Dam (later renamed Buchanan).

The LCRA broke ground on Mansfield Dam, which served as the Colorado River Valley's flood-control structure.

The Texas legislature created the San Antonio River Authority (SARA) with a jurisdiction that included Bexar, Wilson, Karnes, and Goliad counties.

Pres. Franklin D. Roosevelt introduced the Shelterbelt Project in an attempt to help protect land from soil erosion. The project called for large-scale planting of trees across the Great Plains. Farmers were paid to plant and cultivate trees along fencerows separating properties. The intentional planting of the invasive tamarisk (salt cedar) species to protect stream banks and control erosion has led to its establishment over as much as a million acres of floodplains, riparian areas, wetlands, and lake margins in Texas and other parts of the western United States. The tamarisk is an undesirable species because it crowds out native vegetation, increases the salinity of surface soil, and lowers surface water tables.

1938   The LCRA completed construction of Inks Dam, located immediately downstream from Buchanan Dam.

The LCRA board of directors approved the installation of 50 rain gauges, which initiated the first comprehensive watershed reporting system in Texas.

The BRA began construction of its first dam and reservoir project, Possum Kingdom, on the main channel of the Brazos River in Palo Pinto County.

1939   The U.S. Congress expanded the mandate of the USACE to incorporate the construction of water supply and multipurpose flood-control projects.

1940   The LCRA completed reconstruction of Austin Dam (later renamed the Tom Miller Dam), which was owned by the city of Austin. Floods had twice destroyed the dam.

1941   The LCRA completed construction of the Marshall Ford Dam (now the Mansfield Dam).

1944   A U.S.-Mexican treaty committed both countries to the construction of two Rio Grande dams: Falcon and Amistad.

1945   The Texas legislature authorized the Texas Department of Health to enforce drinking water standards for public water supply systems.

1946   Of the 194 electric power plants in Texas, 26 were hydroelectric, generating about 15 percent of the state's electric power.

September floods cost San Antonio six lives and $2.1 million in property damage.

The USACE completed the Barker Dam and Reservoir to provide flood control on Buffalo Bayou in the San Jacinto River Basin for the city of Houston.

1947   The LCRA established a soil conservation program.

Completion of the William Harris Reservoir, an off-channel project between the Brazos River and Oyster Creek, provided an industrial water supply for several plants near Freeport.

1948   Work began on two smaller dams between Inks Dam and Lake Travis to increase the LCRA's hydroelectric capacity. The LCRA completed the Wirtz Dam in 1950 and the Starcke Dam a year later. The term "Highland Lakes" refers to the chain of reservoirs created by the LCRA's six dams.

Of the nearly 30 million acres in Texas agriculture, about 3 million acres were irrigated. Almost 30,000 farms used irrigation systems, including more than 850 farms that used sprinkler or overhead systems.

The Upper Nueces Dam and Reservoir was completed in March and became an important supply of water for the Winter Garden Region.

1949   The Texas legislature declared groundwater to be private property.

The Texas legislature provided for the voluntary establishment of underground water conservation districts.

The Texas legislature divided the Sabine-Neches River Conservation District into the Sabine River Authority of Texas (SRA) and the Neches River Conservation District, renamed Angelina and Neches River Authority (ANRA) in 1977.

More than 4,300 wells irrigated 550,000 acres of agricultural land in the High Plains, El Paso Valley, Winter Garden Region, and Gulf Coast Plains.

In November, Texas entered the historic "drought of record" that lasted for 88 months until March 1957.

1950   "Operation Waterlift" arrived in New York City with 3,000 gallons of water from the Highland Lakes (Buchanan, Inks, LBJ, Marble Falls, Travis, and Austin) to help assist the nation's largest city's drought-stricken residents.

Irrigated land in Texas increased to more than 3 million acres. The growth was mainly from the rapid development of irrigation on the High Plains that was supplied exclusively with high-quality water from the Ogallala Aquifer.

Almost every major river in Texas had at least one dam.

1951   The LCRA's Granite Shoals Dam and Marble Falls Dam (now Starcke Dam) began operation.

The USACE completed Lake Whitney on the Brazos River in Hill, Bosque, and Johnson counties.

The USACE completed its study of the San Antonio River Basin. The Corps recommended 31 miles of improvements along the San Antonio River and its tributaries and the channelization of 2.1 miles of Escondido Creek.

1952   The Briscoe Irrigation Company and the Galveston County Water Company filed complaints with the Texas Railroad Commission regarding the salt pollution resulting from oil and gas operations in the upper Brazos River watershed.

Tropical storms dropped an excess of 30 inches of rain in the Texas Hill Country, which caused record floods on the Pedernales River.

1953   The "drought of record" continued with three-quarters of Texas recording below-average rainfall amounts.

Excessive temperatures roasted Texas cities, for example, Dallas had 52 days with temperatures of 100°F or more.

The Texas legislature created, within the Department of Health, the Texas Water Pollution Control Advisory Council, which became the first state agency responsible for addressing pollution issues.

Presidents Dwight D. Eisenhower and Aldolfo Ruiz Cortines dedicated Falcon Dam located 50 miles downstream from Laredo.

The USACE completed the construction of San Angelo Lake (now O. C. Fisher Lake) and Dam on the North Concho River. The lake serves as a secondary water source and protects San Angelo and other areas below the dam from flooding.

1954   The USACE completed construction of Lake Belton on the Leon River in Bell County.

1955   The Texas legislature created the Trinity River Authority (TRA).

1956   Congress passed the Federal Water Pollution Control Act amendments.

1957   The Texas legislature established the Texas Water Development Board (TWDB) with a mission to predict water supply needs and to provide grant funding for water supply and conservation projects.

In June, Hurricane Audrey swept across the Gulf Coast near the Texas-Louisiana border. In Texas, 9 people died and 450 were injured. Property damage, especially extensive in Jefferson and Orange counties, totaled $8 million.

Drought ended in Central Texas as spring thunderstorms flooded more than 3 million acre-feet of water into the Colorado River.

The TRA established the Central Regional Wastewater System, and its original 28-mile pipeline had expanded to more than 200 miles and served almost 1 million people.

1958   Construction began on the GBRA Canyon Dam on the Guadalupe River to provide flood control and water conservation.

Texas courts, in *Southwest Weather Research, Inc. v. Duncan*, temporarily enjoined cloud seeders from engaging in hail suppression over plaintiffs' lands because of claims of reduced precipitation.

1959   In December, the TRA Central Regional Treatment Plant operations began to serve four member cities—Irving, Grand Prairie, Farmers Branch, and a portion of western Dallas.

The Texas legislature created the Red River Authority (RRA), which included all or part of 43 Texas counties in the watershed of the Red River and its tributaries upstream from Bowie County.

The Texas legislature established the Edwards Underground Water District (EUWD), encompassing five of the six counties in the Edwards Aquifer Recharge Zone.

1960   The LCRA purchased the Gulf Coast Water Company in Bay City and began management of irrigation operations in Matagorda and Wharton counties.

Completion of the SRA Texas Iron Bridge Dam and Lake Tawakoni Reservoir Project in October provided the city of Dallas water for municipal and industrial activities.

1961   The Texas Pollution Control Act eliminated the Water Pollution Advisory Council and created the Texas Water Pollution Board.

An advisory group for water well drillers was established.

The Texas legislature passed the Injection Well Act, which authorized the Texas Board of Water Engineers to regulate waste disposal into the subsurface through injection wells for all but oil and gas industries.

A Texas A&M University study concluded that extensive (underlying parts of Texas, New Mexico, Oklahoma, Arkansas, and Kansas) Permian-aged subterranean salt formations caused contamination in the upper Brazos River Basin.

The Texas legislature expanded SARA's responsibilities to preserve, protect, and manage the resources and ecosystems of the San Antonio River Basin.

In September, Hurricane Carla, the largest hurricane of record in Texas, hit the Gulf Coast. During the storm, a tornado ravaged Galveston Island. The damage to property and crops totaled over $300 million with the heaviest losses sustained in the area between Corpus Christi and Port Arthur. The evacuation of 250,000 people from the coastal region saved many; however, 34 died and 465 were injured.

Texas courts determined in *State v. Valmont Plantations* that irrigation and other major water use rights did not accrue from Spanish and pre-1840 republic land grants unless expressly mentioned.

The Texas legislature prohibited the establishment of additional water districts except for water control and improvement and underground water conservation districts.

1962   The Texas Board of Water Engineers became the Texas Water Commission, which was responsible for water conservation and pollution control and the administration and management of water district activities.

The Texas Water Pollution Board adopted its first rules and regulations.

1963   In April, the SRA and the Sabine River Authority in Louisiana began construction of the Toledo Bend Dam and Reservoir and accompanying power plant. Toledo Bend Reservoir is the largest artificial body of water in the South and fifth largest in surface acres in the United States, having water normally covering an area of 185,000 acres and a controlled storage capacity of 4,477,000 acre-feet.

The USACE completed Lake Proctor on the Leon River in Comanche County.

The United States and Mexico signed the Chamizal Treaty to settle the famous Chamizal dispute. The United States ceded 437 acres in downtown El Paso to Mexico. The treaty provided that the Rio Grande in the El Paso metro be forced through a concrete channel to prevent the river and the international border from changing.

The Texas legislature consolidated the operations of the Texas Game and Fish Commission and the State Parks Board and established the Texas Parks and Wildlife Department (TPWD).

In the case of *Harris County Fresh Water Supply District, No. 55 v. Carr,* the courts determined that the prohibition of creating certain types of water districts was unconstitutional.

1965   The U.S. Congress passed the Federal Water Resources Planning Act.

The Texas Water Commission became the Texas Water Rights Commission, and the TWDB became responsible for functions not related to water rights.

The Water Well Drillers Act established the Water Well Drillers Board.

The Sam Rayburn Dam and Reservoir was completed near Jasper. The resulting lake was 60 miles long with more than 750 miles of shoreline, making it the largest body of water completely within Texas.

In conjunction with Lady Bird Johnson's nationwide beautification campaign, Pres. Lyndon B. Johnson passed the Highway Beautification Act. To help conserve water, Lady Bird Johnson encouraged planting native vegetation.

The USACE completed Lake Waco on the Bosque River in McLennan County.

Lake Granite Shoals, created by Wirtz Dam, was renamed in honor of Pres. Lyndon B. Johnson.

The LCRA's first steam power plant began operation in Bastrop County.

1966   The BRA began construction of the De Cordova Bend Dam and Lake Granbury in Hood County.

Texas had more than 793 water districts. Types of districts included water control and improvement, municipal, water improvement, water supply, conservation and reclamation, irrigation, levee improvement, water control and preservation, drainage, navigation, and waterpower.

1967   The Texas Water Quality Act established the Texas Water Quality Board (TWQB), which assumed all functions of the Water Pollution Control Board and created its first rules.

Twenty-three Texas hydroelectric plants had a total capacity of 390 megawatts.

The USACE completed Lake Somerville on Yegua Creek in Burleson and Washington counties.

In September, the third-largest hurricane of the twentieth century, Hurricane Beulah, swept across South Texas. Beulah spawned 115 tornadoes, and its rains flooded a large part of South Texas for over two weeks. Twenty-four South Texas counties were declared federal disaster areas. Property damage estimates were as high as $100 million, including 3,000 homes that were heavily damage or destroyed, and the storm caused $50 million in crop damage. The evacuation of approximately 300,000 people did not spare 18 people from death and 9,000 others from injury or sickness.

The Texas legislature passed the Water Rights Adjudication Act to quantify water use and to coordinate the administration and management of surface water resources in the state.

1968 The Texas Water Orientated Database was created for providing basic water data to state agencies and the public and later became the Texas Natural Resources Information Service (TNRIS).

Completion of the Roy Clark Reservoir from the impoundment of a tributary of Big Blue Creek 5 miles southwest of Dumas, Moore County, provided an irrigation water supply.

The USACE completed Lake Stillhouse Hollow on the Lampasas River in Bell County.

1969 The Texas Solid Waste Disposal Act empowered the TWQB to regulate industrial solid waste and granted the Texas Department of Health authority to regulate municipal solid waste.

A presidential order created the federal Environmental Protection Agency (EPA).

The De Cordova Bend Dam and Lake Granbury on the Brazos River in Hood County were completed.

Completion of the Amistad Dam and Reservoir took place in November. The United States and Mexico together own the reservoir and dam, and the International Boundary and Water Commission operates the facility. Amistad means "friendship" in Spanish and symbolizes the cooperative spirit both countries exhibited during the project.

Texas' original water plan was presented.

1970 A treaty between the United States and Mexico resolved the boundary at the twin cities of Ojinaga and Presidio and created a 15-mile international floodway.

Hurricane Celia ravaged Corpus Christi in August, killing 13 people and causing damage to commercial buildings, homes, and automobiles in excess of $500 million.

1970s Texas' major hydroelectric power plants included the international Falcon Reservoir and Amistad Dam, both on the Rio Grande; the six Highland Lakes of the Colorado River; the two Brazos River dams; the six Guadalupe River plants; the Red River's Denison Dam; and the Sabine River's Toledo Bend Reservoir.

1971 The Texas legislature authorized the creation of municipal utility districts.

The Texas legislature granted the LCRA the power to control surface water and groundwater pollution, own and operate facilities that provide waste disposal services, manage and develop parks, and encourage fish preservation.

1972 The U.S. Congress passed the Federal Clean Water Act, which requires standards for all point source discharges into receiving water bodies. The law requires a minimum of secondary treatment for all municipal sewage water.

1973 Texas author Elmer Kelton published his award-winning novel, *The Time It Never Rained*, which depicted the struggle of a Texas ranching family to survive the extreme droughts of the 1950s on the Edwards Plateau.

The Texas Parks and Wildlife Department adopted and implemented the Texas Endangered Species Act.

1974 The U.S. Congress enacted the Safe Drinking Water Act.

The New Braunfels Comal power plant closed operations because of financial difficulties.

Approximately 8.5 million acres in Texas were under irrigation. The High Plains region, totaling nearly 5.9 million acres of irrigated agricultural land (65 percent of the Texas total), was one of the largest irrigated areas in the United States.

1975 The Texas legislature allowed the LCRA to develop different types of electric power beyond its traditional hydroelectricity.

The Texas legislature created the Texas Water Trust as a program within the Texas Water Bank for acquiring, by donation, lease, or purchase, water rights for environmental purposes.

Construction began on the SRA Lake Fork Dam and Reservoir to provide industrial and municipal water for the cities of Longview and Dallas.

An interlocal agreement created the Upper Trinity Water Quality Compact to allow for greater capital improvement efforts.

In Austin, the Waterway Development Ordinance, known to some as the Creek Ordinance, set a limit on development in a 100-year floodplain in the metro, thereby protecting the "natural and traditional character" of local creeks.

The problem of excessive pumping of underground water that caused land subsidence, especially in the area between Houston and Galveston, resulted in the creation of the Houston-Galveston Subsidence District, which became the first state agency with powers to restrict groundwater pumping.

1977 The U.S. Congress amended the Federal Clean Water Act to include protection of wetlands.

In an attempt to consolidate the state's water programs, the Texas legislature created the Texas Department of Water Resources (TDWR), retained the TWDB as the policy-making body, renamed the Water Rights Commission as the Texas Water Commission to serve as a quasi-judicial body to rule on permits, and abolished the Texas Water Quality Board.

1978 The GBRA Canyon Dam protected the lower Guadalupe River Basin when 40 inches of rain fell in two days on the upper Guadalupe River. Canyon Lake rose to almost 931 feet above mean sea level, nearly 22 feet above its conservation pool level.

The BRA completed the Sterling C. Robertson Dam, the BRA's third reservoir project, which impounded the Navasota River to form Lake Limestone.

In Medina County, the EUWD constructed two recharge dams, the Middle Verde Creek Dam and the San Geronimo Creek Dam.

The GBRA began construction on the Coleto Creek Park and Reservoir between Goliad and Victoria to become a cooling pond for a coal-fired power plant.

The USACE completed Lake Granger and Lake Georgetown on the San Gabriel River in Williamson County.

The SRA completed the Lake Fork Dam and Reservoir to conserve water for municipal and industrial usages.

In August, Hurricane Allen and its 29 tornadoes roared through Texas, striking Corpus Christi and Padre Island especially hard. More than 250,000 residents evacuated, and 3 people died. Property damage assessments reached $750 million.

1981 The SRA and the city of Dallas signed a contract to move water to the Dallas Water Utilities Eastside Water Treatment Plant from Lake Fork Reservoir.

1982 The LCRA began testing the water quality of the Colorado River.

The City of Corpus Christi and the NRA began construction of the Choke Canyon Reservoir on the Frio River in Live Oak County. The city of Corpus Christi operates the project, which is an industrial and municipal water source for the Coastal Bend area.

The EUWD constructed the Seco Creek Dam in Medina County to enhance recharge to the Edwards Aquifer.

1983 The LCRA purchased the Lakeside Irrigation Company in Colorado County and began managing the company's irrigation canals.

The USACE completed Lake Aquilla on Hackberry and Aquilla creeks in Hill County.

The Texas legislature passed the Wildlife Conservation Act, which gave management authority to the Parks and Wildlife Commission regarding wildlife and fish resources throughout the state.

In August, Hurricane Alicia, with its 32 tornadoes, cut a path through Galveston and Houston and caused 18 deaths, injured 1,800 people, and destroyed or damaged $3 billion in property.

1984 A revised Texas Water Plan addressed future demand for water by identifying conservation strategies for increasing water resources.

The EUWD constructed the Parker Creek Dam in Medina County to improve recharge.

1985 The dissolution of the Department of Water Resources transferred regulatory enforcement to the Texas Water Commission. The re-created Texas Water Development Board assumed planning and finance responsibilities.

The Texas legislature moved the Water Rates and Utilities Services Program to the Texas Water Commission.

Conservation of water, which was recognized as being more economical than developing new sources of water, became a key factor for granting water permits by the Texas legislature.

The Freshwater Inflows Act underscored the need for the consideration of freshwater inflows to bays and estuaries when granting river water permits;

however, minimum amounts of freshwater were not specified.

The Groundwater Act placed construction spacing and size restrictions in critical groundwater areas, regulated nondomestic and nonlivestock water use, and levied property taxes.

Mid- to Late 1980s
About 5.3 million acre-feet of water per year recharged into Texas aquifers, and about 11 million acre-feet of water was withdrawn annually.

1986
Congress amended the Federal Safe Drinking Water Act.

1987
The U.S. Congress passed the Federal Water Quality Act intending to reduce nonpoint source water pollution.

The Wellhead Protection Program, approved by the EPA, was initiated in Texas.

The EUWD developed the state's first regionwide Drought Management Plan.

The provision of water to industrial, municipal, and agricultural users involved over 5,000 local agencies and corporations.

1988
The LCRA began supporting the Colorado River Watch Network with its 500 volunteers, who collected water data along the river and its tributaries and provided environmental education to people in the watershed.

Construction began on two tunnels under downtown San Antonio to diminish the risk of flooding the Paseo del Rio.

In September, Hurricane Gilbert and its 29 tornadoes stormed through Cameron County and caused one death and $5 million in losses.

1989
The Texas legislature expanded the Petroleum Storage Tank program.

In February, the GBRA began operations of the Canyon Dam hydroelectric facility on the Guadalupe River, thereby providing New Braunfels Utilities with a new source of electricity.

The Texas legislature clarified the LCRA's right to conduct conservation programs of water and energy.

The EUWD began the first regionwide municipal leak-detection program in south-central Texas at no charge to cities and water distribution systems.

1990
More than half the water used in the state came from underground sources and was distributed as follows: 71 percent agricultural, 21 percent municipal, and 7 percent industrial.

1991
A special session of the legislature created the Texas Natural Resource Conservation Commission (TNRCC) by consolidating the Texas Air Control Board and the Texas Water Commission.

The Texas Clean Rivers Act established a state program to reduce nonpoint source water pollution.

Guided by the U.S. Clean Rivers Act, the LCRA comprehensively assessed the region's water quality. The TNRCC directed the LCRA to assess the entire Colorado River watershed biennially.

The southern High Plains region had 68 percent of the total irrigated acres in Texas, an irrigated area that had decreased to 6 million acres.

The LCRA established the Colorado River Trail Program, which increased public access to the river and encouraged people to visit the basin's historic communities.

The Living Waters Artesian Springs Catfish Farm in southern Bexar County began operations. Using the principle of right of capture, the owner drilled the world's largest water well (30 inches in diameter and capable of producing 40,000 gallons per minute) and built the infrastructure for the aquaculture project. However, the catfish farm closed after a year because of the lack of a permit to discharge wastewater into the Medina River.

The Texas legislature repealed the statutory provision prohibiting the TWDB from planning interbasin transfers of water to meet future demands.

1992
The LCRA began operation of the Camp Swift Regional Wastewater Project near Bastrop and launched the Buchanan Dam Water Treatment Project.

Only 1 percent of the 420 generating units (30 located out of state) supplying power to Texas were hydroelectric in 1992.

San Antonio's municipal water and wastewater utility, San Antonio Water System (SAWS), was formed from the consolidation of the Alamo Water Conservation and Re-use District, the City Water Board, the City Planning Department's water planning program, and the City Wastewater Department.

The Texas General Land Office managed 20.5 million acres of mineral-right properties and state lands, including submerged lands extending more than 10 miles from the Texas coast into the Gulf of Mexico.

The Texas Water Commission declared the Edwards Aquifer to be an underground river; however, the Texas Supreme Court ruled this attempt to regulate the Edwards Aquifer unconstitutional.

1993   The Texas legislature created the Edwards Aquifer Authority (EAA) in response to a federal court ruling requiring limits on groundwater pumped from the aquifer to ensure adequate continuous flows from the aquifer's two main springs—Comal Springs in New Braunfels and San Marcos Springs in San Marcos, which are two of the most plentiful springs in the United States and home to endangered aquatic species.

The TNRCC brought together regulatory programs for water, air, and waste within one agency.

1994   Twenty-three hydroelectric power plants operated in Texas with a combined potential generation of 541.7 megawatts (less than 2 percent of total electricity capacity of Texas).

The BRA completed Lake Alan Henry in Kent and Garza counties to serve the city of Lubbock.

San Antonio voters rejected the proposal for building the Applewhite Reservoir, a surface water supply reservoir to assist with the city's growing water demands.

1995   The LCRA developed wind-generated electricity for commercial use and became one of Texas' largest renewable energy providers with its water- and wind-power network.

The Sandy Creek Memorial Day flood caused the National Weather Service and the LCRA to cooperate in placing NOAA Weather Radio transmitters in the area.

The TNRCC recognized TRA's Central Regional Wastewater Treatment System as the state's best large wastewater treatment plant.

The BRA and LCRA created the Brazos-Colorado Water Agency to address water and wastewater concerns in the rapidly growing Williamson County area.

Construction was completed on the San Pedro Creek flood bypass tunnel (24 feet in diameter and 6,000 feet in length) beneath the city of San Antonio.

1996   The U.S. Congress reauthorized the Federal Safe Drinking Water Act.

The Texas Supreme Court unanimously overturned a district court decision declaring the EAA Act unconstitutional, thereby dissolving the EUWD and facilitating management of the San Antonio section of the Edwards Aquifer.

The EAA mandated that all municipal, industrial, and agricultural users of the Edwards Aquifer were required to file a declaration of historical use and request an initial permit by December 31.

The EAA directors adopted interim Critical Period Management Rules that set new water conservation triggers and stages with the goal of slowing the decline of spring flows during droughts.

The Living Waters Artesian Springs Catfish Farm in southern Bexar County reopened, using only 2 percent of the previous flow and constructing a holding pond designed to retain all the water used on the property. These measures negated the need for a discharge permit. The EAA asserted, however, that the design of the holding pond was faulty and that water was still being discharged to the Medina River illegally. The catfish farm shut down once again.

In February, the Ozarka Spring Water Company began pumping 90,000 gallons per day from the Carrizo-Wilcox Aquifer in Henderson County. Within days, an adjacent continuously flowing, 100-year-old well went dry. Eventually, wells in other nearby properties went dry, leading to legal action that the Texas Supreme Court would resolve in 1999.

1997   The Texas legislature transferred regulation of water well drillers from the TNRCC to the Texas Department of Licensing and Regulation.

In reaction to the severe drought in 1996, the Texas legislature adopted Senate Bill 1, "The Water Bill," which mandated water conservation planning for large water users, required public water suppliers to draft drought contingency plans, and limited interbasin transfers.

The LCRA contained the June flood within the Colorado River floodplains, although floodwaters caused $4 million in damage at Lake Marble Falls.

Various federal and state agencies collaborated in conducting the Middle Brazos Reconnaissance Study to determine the natural resources lost because of the changes in land use in the North Bosque River watershed and other watersheds in the middle Brazos River basin and to develop appropriate restorative measures.

The NRA and the city of Corpus Christi collaborated to construct the Mary Rhodes Memorial Pipeline (101 miles long and 5 feet in diameter) to carry water from Lake Texana in Jackson County to Nueces County's Corpus Christi treatment facilities.

1998   The LCRA purchased the Garwood Irrigation Company, holder of the largest block of privately held Colorado River water rights.

The LCRA opened the McKinney Roughs Nature Park, a 1,600-acre ecological showcase between Bastrop and Austin.

Tropical Storm Charley ripped across the lower Rio Grande Basin and caused 13 deaths and $50 million in damages.

In only a few hours, 30 inches of rainfall in Central Texas triggered flash flooding of the Guadalupe and Colorado river basins, resulting in 29 deaths and $750 million in property damage.

1999   The LCRA and the city of Austin signed an agreement ensuring adequate water supplies for the city for the next 50 years.

The LCRA purchased the last remaining block, the Pierce Ranch, of the Colorado River Basin's privately held water rights.

The BRA purchased the Allen's Creek Reservoir site from Reliant Energy.

The Texas legislature passed Senate Bill 1911 to create county-based groundwater conservation districts that can regulate groundwater use and collect fees.

The Texas Supreme Court, in *Sipriano v. Ozarka Spring Water Co.*, ruled that even though the Sipriano family had presented compelling reasons for the regulation of groundwater use, it was inappropriate for the court to substitute the rule of reasonable use for the historical rule of capture.

2000   The Texas legislature directed the TNRCC to change its name to the Texas Commission on Environmental Quality (TCEQ) by January 1, 2004.

The San Marcos River Foundation filed an application with the TNRCC for water permits for 1.3 million acre-feet of water from the San Marcos and Guadalupe rivers for in-stream habitat and freshwater inflows into San Antonio Bay.

In December, SAWS paid $9 million for Living Waters Artesian Springs Catfish Farm in southern Bexar County, as well as most of its water rights, which added 10,000 acre-feet of pumping rights to the city of San Antonio.

2001   In October, the GBRA's Lockhart Water Treatment Plant began pumping water with high iron concentrations from the Carrizo Aquifer for the city.

To counter abnormally high wastewater flows, the ANRA approved plans to develop the North Angelina County Regional Wastewater Facility.

The SARA, GBRA, and SAWS entered into an agreement to transfer 70,000 acre-feet of water yearly to San Antonio from the Guadalupe River.

The Texas legislature passed Senate Bill 2, which gave groundwater conservation districts the right to limit new groundwater wells if such wells would threaten historic users of an aquifer.

Tropical Storm Allison dropped more than 20 inches of rain on downtown Houston and caused widespread flooding and disruption.

2002   The TNRCC officially became the TCEQ on September 1.

In February, the LCRA and SAWS agreed to share water resources in the lower Colorado River Basin and the San Antonio area. SAWS also began to obtain water from the Trinity Aquifer.

The TWDB's State Water Plan obligated state funding for development of water resources and became the first comprehensive statewide water management plan.

The State Water Plan listed 99 existing Texas interbasin transfers and recommended the voluntary development of East Texas surface water transfers to meet the projected water needs until 2050 for the San Jacinto River Authority, the Gulf Coast Water Authority, the Brazos River Authority, and Williamson County.

The State Water Plan provided for the establishment of county-based groundwater districts with the authority to limit pumping by new permit holders.

Tropical storms in June and July dropped up to 40 inches of rain on the Hill Country, causing Canyon Dam on the Guadalupe River to spill over and produce widespread downstream flood damage.

In August, the GBRA Hays-Caldwell Water Ultrafiltration Membrane Treatment Plant in Caldwell County near San Marcos started operation with a capacity of 2 million gallons per day.

The EAA and Living Waters Artesian Springs, Ltd. (former catfish farm), reached a compromise settlement that provided an initial regular permit for the company to draw 22,500 acre-feet annually from the Edwards Aquifer.

2003   In December, SAWS purchased the remaining tangible assets of Living Waters Artesian Springs, Ltd., including its well, and an additional 3,125 acre-feet in water rights. The sale left the company with 9,375 acre-feet in water rights. Overall, SAWS paid Living Waters Artesian Springs more than $30 million for water sales, leases, land, and equipment.

2004   An agreement between the GBRA and SAWS allowed the northwest portion of San Antonio to receive 3,000 acre-feet of Canyon Lake water annually.

2005   Category 5 Hurricane Rita forced mass evacuation of more than 1 million residents from the southeast Texas coast. The storm weakened before driving inland at the Texas-Louisiana border.

Glossary

acre-foot: The amount of water required to cover an area of 1 acre (43,560 square feet) to a depth of 1 foot that totals 43,560 cubic feet or 325,851 gallons.

aquiclude: A rock or sedimentary unit of low transmissivity that precludes the flow of groundwater.

aquifer: A body of rock or sediment that contains water that can be withdrawn.

artesian well: A well in which the water is under hydrostatic pressure and may flow without pumping.

bay: A body of water that is partially enclosed by land with a wide opening to the ocean.

bayou: A term given to a slow-moving stream that meanders across a flat coastal plain in parts of the American South.

brackish water: Water that has greater than 1,000 parts per million (ppm) dissolved salts but less than the 34,000 ppm salinity of ocean water.

climate: The long-term weather characteristics and phenomena for a location. The U.S. National Weather Service uses decadal 30-year averages, such as 1971–2000, to describe the climate for sites in the United States.

cubic feet per second (cfs or ft³/sec or ft³s⁻¹): The rate of flow of a stream that is equal to the width times the averaged depth times the average velocity of a stream ($W \times D \times V$). One cubic foot of water is equal to 7.48 gallons, which means that a stream flowing at the rate of 1 cfs is flowing at the rate of 7.48 gallons per second. Many Texas streams with a long-term average flow of 200 to 300 cfs or less have record floods of greater than 100,000 cfs or 748,000 gallons per second.

desalination: The process of removing dissolved materials, "salts," from brackish or oceanic water. The two major methods are "flash distillation," which is essentially boiling the salty water and capturing the condensing steam, and "reverse osmosis," which entails forcing the salty water through a semipermeable membrane under great pressure.

ecosystem: The assemblage of plants and animals (biota) in a particular habitat.

endangered species: Species whose survival is at risk of extinction. Federal and state governments prescribe procedures for characterizing a species as "endangered," thereby giving the species and its critical habitat legal protection.

escarpment: A steep drop-off from an elevated landscape. One of the most famous escarpments in Texas is the Balcones Escarpment in Central Texas, which breaks the Edwards Aquifer to form the Texas "spring line" from Waco to Del Rio. Another famous Texas escarpment is the Caprock Escarpment, which forms the eastern edge between the High Plains and the Llano Estacado in the Panhandle.

estuary: To geographers and geologists, an estuary is the flooded lower reaches of a river valley caused by the rise in sea level since the last glacial maximum 18,000 years ago. To a biologist, an estuary is a zone of mixing of fresh and marine waters so that the water has less than ocean salinity—critical for the survival of the juvenile forms of many economically and environmentally significant species, such as blue crabs, shrimp, and redfish. Most geographic/geologic estuaries are estuaries to biologists, but many biological estuaries are not geographic/geologic estuaries and are other water bodies that are isolated from the open ocean, such as lagoons and bays, but not necessarily drowned river valleys.

eustasy: The uniform worldwide change in sea level caused by a change in the volume of the oceans. The major cause of eustasy over the past 3 million years has been the uptake of the ocean's waters to form glaciers during the Pleistocene glaciations ("ice ages"), resulting in a drop of sea level as much as 400 feet below the present-day level. Global warming today is melting the world's glaciers and causing thermal expansion of the ocean's waters that produces a rise in sea level.

evapotranspiration: The transfer of liquid water from the soil to water vapor in the atmosphere through the process of evaporation from the soil or transpiration through plants. Generally, the hotter and drier the climate, the greater will be the potential for evapotranspiration.

fault line: A break in the earth's surface caused by seismic forces within the earth.

floodplain: The region adjacent to the channel of a stream that is periodically flooded during high flow conditions. A "100-year" floodplain is a floodplain that has a 1 percent chance of being flooded in any given year. A "500-year" floodplain is an area that has a 0.2 percent chance of being flooded in any given year.

groundwater: Water below the land surface contained in saturated rocks or sediment that can be withdrawn for human use.

hurricane: A tropical cyclonic storm with winds greater than 74 miles per hour in the Atlantic Ocean, Caribbean Sea, and Gulf of Mexico. Similar storms are also known as *chubascos* off the west coast of Mexico, as *typhoons* in the western Pacific Ocean, and as *cyclones* in the Indian Ocean.

inflow: The flow of water into a water body, for example, the flow of freshwater into the ocean at biological estuaries that is responsible for the reduced salinity necessary for the survival of the juvenile stages of many marine animals.

interbasin transfer: The transfer of surface water from one drainage basin to another. Interbasin transfer usually entails transferring water from a basin in which all of the water is not allocated to a basin.

karst: The landforms, landform processes, and hydrologic characteristics of soluble rocks such as limestone, dolomite, gypsum, and marble. Notable features include caves and caverns below the surface and sinkholes and springs at the surface.

leachate: A solution of dissolved substances that has percolated through soil or landfills.

marsh: A grassy or herbaceous area that is underlain by water-saturated soil.

millions of gallons per day (MGD): A term used by municipalities and other water resource utilities for daily water use and daily wastewater production. In Texas, per person residential urban water use ranges from 140 gallons per day to more than 300 gallons per day.

recharge zone: The land area where significant amounts of surface water enter an aquifer. Recharge may come from either infiltration of soil water or water that sinks into the bed of a stream that is above the level of the water table of the aquifer.

relief: Differences in elevation of the land surface.

rule of capture: The legal principle that allows a person to use as much water as can be withdrawn as long as it is for a beneficial use. The 1904 *Houston RR v. East* case initially confirmed this principle for Texas groundwater law, and the 1999 *Sipriano v. Ozarka Spring Water Co.* case reaffirmed its legality.

spring: A point where groundwater naturally flows onto the surface or into a surface water body.

stream: A watercourse with a defined bed and banks, which does not necessarily have to convey water at all times. Texas water law mandates that water in a stream is confined water and is thus owned by the citizens of the state.

subsidence: The lowering of the land surface due to the withdrawal of subsurface materials such as water, oil, coal, or mineral ores.

surface water: Water on the land surface as opposed to groundwater, which is below the surface. Surface water can be either confined as in a stream channel or unconfined as in the surface runoff or "overland flow" before the water enters a defined stream channel.

swamp: A wetland covered predominantly with trees.

total maximum daily load (TMDL): The maximum amount of a particular pollutant that can be added to a water body and still meet the minimum acceptable water quality standards.

transmissivity: The rate at which water flows through rocks or sediment.

vadose: The unsaturated zone of the earth above the permanent groundwater level.

water mining: The withdrawal of water from an aquifer at a rate greater than the long-term rate of recharge, which results in a lowering of the water table and is sometimes associated with problems such as land subsidence, earth fissures, and decrease in water quality.

wetland: A water-saturated area, such as a marsh, swamp, or bog, that supports a habitat dependent on saturated soil conditions. Since passage of the federal 1977 Clean Water Act, wetlands have been legally protected because of their ability to improve water quality and absorb floodwaters.

Acronyms

BRA	Brazos River Authority
CSC	Coastal Services Center
EAA	Edwards Aquifer Authority
EPA	U.S. Environmental Protection Agency
EUWD	Edwards Underground Water District
FCWA	Federal Clean Water Act
GBRA	Guadalupe-Blanco River Authority
GLO	General Land Office
LCRA	Lower Colorado River Authority
NCDC	National Climate Data Center
NOAA	National Oceanographic and Atmospheric Administration
NPS	National Park Service
NRA	Nueces River Authority
NWS	National Weather Service
RCT	Railroad Commission of Texas
RRA	Red River Authority
SARA	San Antonio River Authority
SAWS	San Antonio Water System
SRA	Sabine River Authority of Texas
TCEQ	Texas Commission on Environmental Quality
TNRIS	Texas Natural Resource Information Service
TPWD	Texas Parks and Wildlife Department
TRA	Trinity River Authority
TWDB	Texas Water Development Board
TWPD	Texas Parks and Wildlife Department
USACE	U.S. Army Corps of Engineers
USDOE	U.S. Department of Energy
USFS	U.S. Forest Service
USFWS	U.S. Fish and Wildlife Service
USGS	U.S. Geological Survey

References

About. 2004–2006. http://www.about.com/ (accessed June 2004–January 2006).

American Sportfishing Association. 2002. http://www.asafishing.org/asa/statistics/index.html (accessed August 2006).

AmericanZoos.com. 2006. http://www.americanzoos.com/ (accessed July 2005–August 2006).

Angelina and Neches River Authority (ANRA). 2004. http://www.anra.org/ (accessed June 2004).

Austin American-Statesman. 2006. http://www.senate.state.tx.us/SRC/pdf/SL-TxDrought-web.pdf#search=%22austin%20american-statesman%20drought%202006%22 (accessed August 2006).

Beaumont, P. 1985. Irrigated agriculture and ground-water mining on the High Plains of Texas, USA. *Environmental Conservation* 12:119–30.

Besse, Helen. 2007. Letter. Correspondence about Texas springs. January 2.

Boldt-Van Rooy, T. 2003. Bottling up our natural resources: The fight over bottled water extraction in the United States. *Journal of Land Use* 18:268–98.

Bomar, G. W. 1995. *Texas weather.* 2d ed. Austin: University of Texas Press.

Brazos River Authority (BRA). 2004–2005. http://www.brazos.org/ (accessed June 2004–January 2005).

Britton, J. C., and B. Morton. 1998. *Shore ecology of the Gulf of Mexico.* 2d ed. Austin: University of Texas Press.

Brune, Gunnar. 2002. *The springs of Texas.* 2d ed. College Station: Texas A&M University Press.

Bureau of Economic Geology. 2004–2006. http://www.beg.utexas.edu/ (accessed June 2004–January 2006).

Canadian River Municipal Authority (CRMWA). 2004–2005. http://www.crmwa.com/ (accessed June 2004–January 2005).

Canyon Lake Times Guardian. 2001. San Antonio pipeline to draw 70,000 acre-feet of water per year from Guadalupe River by 2010/SAWS, GBRA, SARA ink water deal for 23 billion gallons of water from downstream, May 23. http://www.timesguardian.com/news/5–23pipelineGuadalupe.html (accessed June 2004).

Carpenter, Alan T. 1998. Element stewardship abstract for tamarisk. The Nature Conservancy. http://nature.org/ (accessed June 2004).

Cech, T. V. 2005. *Principles of water resources: History, development, management, and policy.* 2d ed. New York: John Wiley.

Chowdhury, A. H., C. Ridgeway, and R. E. Mace. 2004. Origin of the waters in San Solomon Spring System, Trans-Pecos Texas. In *Aquifers of the Edwards Plateau,* edited by R. E. Mace, E. S. Angle, and W. F. Mullican III. Texas Water Development Board Report 360, 315–44. Austin: Texas Water Development Board.

City of Corpus Christi. 2004–2005. http://www.cctexas.com/ (accessed June 2004–January 2005).

City of San Marcos Texas Water and Wastewater. 2004–2006. http://www.ci.san-marcos.tx.us/ departments/WWW (accessed June 2004–January 2006).

Coastal Services Center. 2004–2006. National Oceanic and Atmospheric Administration (NOAA) http://www.csc.noaa.gov/ (accessed June 2004–January 2006).

Corbitt, R. A. 1999. *Standard handbook of environmental engineering.* 2d ed. New York: McGraw-Hill.

de la Teja, Jesus F. 1995. *San Antonio de Bexar.* Albuquerque: University of New Mexico Press.

Dingman, S. L. 2002. *Physical hydrology.* 2d ed. Upper Saddle River, N.J.: Prentice Hall.

Dive Texas. 2006. http://www.divetexas.com/ (accessed January 2006).

Dugas, W. A., and C. G. Ainsworth. 1983. *Agroclimatic atlas of Texas.* College Station: Texas Agricultural Experiment Station.

Dunne, T., and L. B. Leopold. 1978. *Water in environmental planning.* San Francisco: W. H. Freeman.

Earl, R. A., R. W. Dixon, and C. A. Day. 2006. Long-term precipitation and water supply variability in south-central Texas. *Proceedings and Papers of the Applied Geography Conferences* 29:11–22.

Earl, R. A., and T. H. Votteler. 2005. Major water issues facing south-central Texas. In *Water for Texas,* edited by J. Norwine, J. R. Giardino, and S. Krishnamurthy, 75–87. College Station: Texas A&M University Press.

Eckhardt, Gregg. 2004. Ron Pucek's Living Waters Catfish Farm. The Edwards Aquifer. http://www.edwardsaquifer.net/pucek.html (accessed June 2004).

Edwards Aquifer Authority (EAA). 2004–2006. http://www.edwardsaquifer.org/ (accessed June 2004–January 2006).

Environmental Systems Research Institute (ESRI). 2002–2006. http://www.esri.com/ (accessed June 2004–January 2006).

Federal Insurance and Mitigation Administration, Federal Emergency Management Administration (FEMA). 2000. http://www.fema.gov/about/ divisions/mitigation/mitigation.shtm (accessed June 2004–January 2006).

Fish, Ernest B., Erin L. Atkinson, Tony R. Mollhagen, Christopher H. Shanks, and Cynthia M. Brenton. 2000. *Playa Lakes Digital Database for the Texas portion of the Playa Lakes Joint Venture Region.* http://library.ttu.edu:80/ul/playa/gis/playa_gis.htm (accessed June 2004–January 2006).

Flood Safety. 2006. *Flood damage and fatality statistics.* www.floodsafety.com/national/life/ statistics.htm (accessed September 2006).

Goudie, A., and J. Wilkinson. 1977. *The warm desert environment.* Cambridge: Cambridge University Press.

Greater San Marcos Economic Development Council. 2000. *San Marcos, Texas community profile.* San Marcos: Greater San Marcos Economic Development Council.

Guadalupe-Blanco River Authority (GBRA). 2004–2006. http://www.gbra.org/ (accessed June 2004–January 2006).

Guerra, Mary Ann Noonan. 1987. *The San Antonio River.* San Antonio: Alamo Press.

Harris-Galveston Subsidence District. 2004–2006. http://www.hgsubsidence.org/ (accessed June 2004–August 2006).

Haywood, C. E. 1995. *Monitoring of aquifer compaction and land subsidence due to ground-water withdrawal in the*

El Paso, Texas-Juarez, Chihuahua area. U.S. Geological Survey Open-File Report 94–0532. Reston, Va.: U.S. Geological Survey.

HDR Engineering. 2001. *South central Texas regional water planning area regional water plan.* Austin: HDR Engineering.

Heitmuller, F. T., and B. D. Reece. 2003. *Database of historically documented springs and spring flow measurements in Texas.* U.S. Geological Survey Open-File Report 03–315. http://pubs.usgs.gov/of/2003/ofr03–315/ (accessed March 2007).

Houck, O. A. 1999. *The Clean Water Act TMDL Program: Law, policy and implementation.* Washington, D.C.: Environmental Law Institute.

Houston Chronicle. 2001. http://www.chron.com/ (accessed June 2004–January 2006).

International Boundary and Water Commission. 2005. http://www.ibwc.state.gov/ (accessed June 2005–January 2006).

Jenson, M. E., R. D. Burman, and R. G. Allen. 1992. *Evapotranspiration and irrigation water requirements.* ASCE manuals and reports on engineering practice, No. 70. New York: American Society of Civil Engineers.

Kaiser, Ronald A. 1987. *Handbook on Texas water law.* Water Monograph No. 87-1. College Station: Texas Water Resources Institute.

———. 1996a. A primer on Texas surface water law for the regional planning process. Texas A&M University. Presented at the Texas Water Law Conference Austin, Texas, October 1, 1998. http://www.bickerstaff.com/waterlawfeature/kaiser.htm#N_74_ (accessed June 2004).

———. 1996b. Texas water marketing in the next millennium: A conceptual and legal analysis. *Texas Tech Law Review* 27:181. http://www.tamu.edu/rakwater/ Pdf/WATER-MARKETING.pdf (accessed June 2004).

Kelton, Elmer. 1973. *The time it never rained.* New York: Doubleday.

Kline, B. 2000. *First along the river: A brief history of the U.S. environmental movement.* 2d ed. San Francisco: Acada Books.

Larkin, Thomas J., and George W. Bomar. 1983. *Climatic atlas of Texas.* Austin: Texas Department of Water Resources.

Leake, S. A. 2004. *Land subsidence from ground-water pumping.* U.S. Geological Survey. http://geochange.er.usgs.gov/sw/changes/anthropogenic/subside/ (accessed June 2004–January 2006).

Legates, D. R. 2004. Climate and water. In *Water for Texas,* edited by J. Norwine, J. R. Giardino, and S. Krishnamurthy, 149–52. College Station: Texas A&M University Press.

Leopold, L. B., Wolman, M. G., and Miller, J. P. 1964. *Fluvial processes in geomorphology.* San Francisco: W. H. Freeman.

Lower Colorado River Authority (LCRA). 1996–2005. http://www.lcra.org (accessed June 2004–July 2006).

———. 2006. http://www.lcra.org/ index.html (accessed January 2006).

Mathewson, Christopher C. 2006. Gulf Coast shoreline erosion: A complex engineering geology problem. Paper presented at the annual meeting of the American Association of Petroleum Geologists, Houston, April; posted as Search and Discovery Article #50031. http://www.searchanddiscovery.net/documents/2006/06056mathewson/index.htm (accessed August 2006).

Minor, Joseph. 1968. *A brief on the acequias of San Antonio.* San Antonio: ASCE.

National Climate Data Center (NCDC). 2000. *Climate atlas of the United States.* Asheville, N.C.: National Oceanic and Atmospheric Administration (NOAA).

———. 2004–2006. National Oceanic and Atmospheric Administration (NOAA) Satellite and Information Service. http://www.ncdc.noaa.gov/oa/ncdc.html (accessed June 2004–January 2006, March 2007).

———. 2006. *Climatological data.* www.ncdc.gov (accessed February 2006).

National Oceanic and Atmospheric Administration (NOAA). 2002–2005. http://www.noaa.gov/ (accessed June 2004–August 2006).

National Oceanic and Atmospheric Administration (NOAA), National Geophysical Data Center (NGDC). 2002–2004. 20th century drought. http://www.ngdc.noaa.gov/paleo/ drought/ drght_ history.html (accessed June 2004).

National Park Service (NPS). 2000–2005. http://www.nps.gov/ (accessed June 2004–January 2006).

National Weather Service. 1959, 2000–2006. National Oceanic and Atmospheric Administration (NOAA). http://www.nws.noaa.gov/ (accessed June 2004–January 2006).

———. 2006. Flood safety. http://www.weather.gov/floodsafety/ (accessed August 2006).

National Wetlands Inventory. 1992. http://www.fws.gov/nwi/ (accessed June 2004–January 2006).

Natural Resource Conservation Service. 2004. U.S. Department of Agriculture. http://www.nrcs.usda.gov/ (accessed June 2004–January 2006).

Norwine, James, John R. Giardino, and Sushma Krishnamurthy, eds. 2005. *Water for Texas.* College Station: Texas A&M University Press.

Nueces River Authority (NRA). 2006. http://www.nueces-ra.org/ (accessed June 2006).

Oliver, James. 2004. Park Ranger, National Park Service, San Antonio Missions. Interview, October 3.

Petersen, James F. 1995. Along the edge of the Hill Country: The Texas spring line. In *A geographic glimpse of Central Texas and the Borderlands,* edited by James F. Petersen and Julie A. Tuason, 20–30. Pathways in Geography Series. Indiana, Penn.: National Council for Geographic Education.

Playa Lakes Joint Venture. 2004. http://www.pljv.org/ (accessed June 2004–January 2006).

Railroad Commission of Texas (RCT). 2003–2006. http://www.rrc.state.tx.us/ (accessed June 2004–January 2006).

Red River Authority (RRA). 2004–2006. http://www.rra.dst.tx.us/ (accessed June 2004–January 2006).

Sabine River Authority (SRA). 2004–2006. http://www.sra.dst.tx.us/ (accessed June 2004–January 2006).

San Antonio Express-News. 1999. http://www.express-news.com/2006/index.php (accessed January 2006).

San Antonio Water System (SAWS). 2004–2006. Planning our water future for the next 50 years. http://www.saws.org/our_water/future/index.shtml (accessed June 2004–January 2006).

Save Our Springs, Inc. 1998–2002. Supreme Court to decide whether Texas landowners are protected from drainage of aquifer. http://www.saveoursprings.com/news/eustance.htm (accessed July 2004).

Shiner, J. L. 1983. Large springs and early American Indians. *Plains Anthropologist* 29:34–36.

Slade, Raymond M., Jr., and John Patton. 2003. *Major and catastrophic storms and floods in Texas.* U.S. Geological Survey Open-File Report 03-193. http://pubs.usgs.gov/of/2003/ofr03–193/cd_files/USGS_Storms/background.htm (accessed August 2006).

Stahle, D. W., and Cleaveland, M. K. 1988. Texas drought history reconstructed and analyzed from 1698 to 1980. *Journal of Climate* 1:59–74.

Supreme Court of Texas. 1999. No. 98-0247: *Bart Sipriano, Harold Fain, and Doris Fain, Petitioners v. Great Spring Waters of America, Inc.* A/K/A Ozarka Natural Spring Water Co. A/K/A Ozarka Spring Water Co. A/K/A Ozarka, Respondents. S.W.3d 75; 1999 Tex. LEXIS 49; 42_ Tex. Sup. J. 629, November 19, 1998, Argued; May 6, 1999, Opinion Delivered. http://www

.detcog.org/groundwaterdistrict/courtbill.pdf (accessed July 2004).

Tarrant County Water Control District. 2005. http://www.trwd .com/ (accessed January 2005).

Texas Agricultural Extension Service. 1998, 2004–2006. Texas A&M University. http://texasextension.tamu.edu/ (accessed June 2004–January 2006).

Texas Bar CLE. 2005. *The changing face of water rights in Texas 2005*. Austin: State Bar of Texas.

Texas Commission on Environmental Quality (TCEQ); formerly Texas Natural Resource Conservation Commission (TNRCC). 2000–2006. http://www.tceq.state.tx.us/ (accessed June 2004–January 2006).

Texas Department of Health Services. 2007. *Fish consumption advisory.* http://www.dshs.state.tx.us/seafood/survey .shtm#advisory (accessed May 2006).

Texas Diver. 2006. http://www.texasdiver.com/ (accessed January 2006).

Texas Environmental Center. 1997 *Texas environmental almanac— online.* http://www.texascenter.org/almanac/ (accessed March 2007).

Texas Environmental Profiles. 2004. http://www.texasep.org/ (accessed June 2004–January 2006).

Texas Natural Resources Information System (TNRIS). 1996– 2002. http://www.tnris.state.tx.us/ (accessed June 2004–January 2006).

Texas Parks and Wildlife Department (TPWD). 2004–2006. http:// www.tpwd.state.tx.us/ (accessed June 2004–January 2006).

Texas Public Utility Commission. 2005. http://www.puc.state.tx.us/ (accessed January 2006).

Texas Secretary of State. 2007. Texas Administrative Code, Title 16, Part 1, Ch. 3, Title 30, Section 1, Ch. 331. http://info.sos .state.tx.us/pls/pub/readtac$ext.viewtac (accessed March 2007).

Texas State Historical Association. 2004–2006. *Handbook of Texas online.* http://www.tsha.utexas.edu/handbook/online/ (accessed June 2004–August 2006).

Texas Strategic Mapping Program (StratMap): Digital Orthophoto Quarter Quadrangle (DOQQ). 2000. http://www.tnris.state.tx .us/stratmap/ (accessed June 2004–January 2006).

Texas Synergy. 2006. The Texas drought. http://synergyx.tacc .utexas.edu/drought_main.html (accessed August 2006).

Texas Water Development Board (TWDB). 1999–2007. http://www .twdb.state.tx.us/home/index.asp (accessed June 2004–August 2006).

———. 2002. *Water for Texas.* http://www.twdb.state.tx.us/ publi- cations/reports/State_Water_Plan/2002/FinalWaterPlan2002.asp (accessed June 2004–January 2006).

———. 2007. *Water for Texas 2007.* www.twdb.state.tx.us (accessed March 2007).

Texas Water Foundation. 2001–2003. Texas water historical time- line. http://texaswater.org/ water/history/default.htm (accessed June 2004).

Texas Water Law Institute. 1997. *Senate Bill 1: A new chapter in Texas water law.* Austin: Texas Water Law Institute.

Thompson, S. A. 1999. *Water use, management, and planning in the United States.* San Diego: Academic Press.

Thornthwaite, C. W. 1948. An approach toward a rational classifi- cation of climate. *Geographical Review* 38:55–94.

Titus, James G., and Charlie Richman. 2001. Maps of lands vulner- able to sea level rise: Modeled elevations along the U.S. Atlantic and Gulf coasts. *Climate Research.* http://yosemite.epa.gov/ oar/globalwarming.nsf/UniqueKeyLookup/SHSU5C3J4E/$File/ maps.pdf (accessed July 2006).

Trinity River Authority (TRA). 2004–2006. http://www.trinityra .org/ (accessed June 2004–January 2006).

Tyler, Ron, ed. 1996. *The new handbook of Texas.* Austin: Texas State Historical Association.

U.S. Army Corps of Engineers (USACE). 2003–2006. http://www .usace.army.mil/ (accessed June 2004–August 2006).

U.S. Bureau of Reclamation. 2005. http://www.usbr.gov/ (accessed June 2004–January 2005).

U.S. Bureau of Transportation Statistics. 2001. http://www.bts.gov/ (accessed June 2004–January 2006).

U.S. Census Bureau. 2000. http://www.census.gov/ (accessed June 2004–January 2006).

———. 2005. Population division, interim state population projec- tions. http://www.census.gov (accessed March 2007).

U.S. Department of Energy, Energy Information Agency (USDOE). 2006. *Inventory of electrical utility power plants.* http://www .eia.doe.gov/cneaf/electricity/ipp/ipp_sum.html (accessed Febru- ary 2006).

U.S. Environmental Protection Agency (EPA). 1999–2006. http:// www.epa.gov/ (accessed June 2004–January 2006).

U.S. Federal Highway Administration. 2001. Memorandum HCC-30: Legal analysis of New Supreme Court case on *Wet- lands, Solid Waste Agency of Northern Cook County v. US Army Corps of Engineers,* No. 99–1178. http://www.fhwa .dot.gov/environment/ wetland/swancclg.htm (accessed March 2007).

U.S. Fish and Wildlife Service (USFWS). 2002–2006. http://www .fws.gov/ (accessed June 2004–August 2006).

U.S. Forest Service (USFS). 2002. http://www.fs.fed.us/ (accessed June 2004–January 2006).

U.S. Geological Survey (USGS). 1994, 1998. http://www.usgs.gov/ (accessed June 2004–January 2006).

———. 1999–2006. http://www.usgs.gov/ (accessed June 2004– January 2006).

U.S. Geological Survey (USGS), National Water Inventory System. 2005. *User's manual for the national water information system of the U.S. Geological Survey.* Open-File Report 2005-1251. http://pubs.usgs.gov/of/2004/1238/ (accessed June 2004– January 2006).

Webb, S. L., C. J. Zabransky, R. S. Lyons, and D. G. Hewitt. 2006. Water quality and summer use of water in Texas. *Southwestern Naturalist* 51:368–75.

WISE Uranium Project. 2004. http://www.wise-uranium.org/ (accessed June 2004–January 2006).

Zoos & Aquariums. 2006. http://www.americanzoos.info/ (accessed June 2004–January 2006).

Index

ISBN-13: 978-1-60344-020-2
ISBN-10: 1-60344-020-8

52495